Emily Brontë, D. H. Lawrence and *the Black Horse*

Emily Brontë, D. H. Lawrence and *the Black Horse*

ASHOK CELLY

PRAGATI PUBLICATIONS
DELHI

PRAGATI PUBLICATIONS
9926 Library Road,
Azad Market, Delhi 110006

First Published 1997

ISBN: 81-7307-046-6

Published by Vinod Kapoor for Pragati Publications
9926 Library Road, Azad Market, Delhi 110006

Typeset and Printed by Vikas Print Communication Services
New Delhi 110026

For Papaji who Loved Books

CONTENTS

Foreword ix

Preface xiii

Acknowledgements xv

1 Through the Maze of Criticism 1

2 Brontë, Lawrence and the Protest against Civilization 13

3 Passion and Cruelty in *Wuthering Heights* 28

4 Lawrence's Rejection of Platonic–Christian Idealism 44

5 Laurentian Alternative: The Non-Humanist Vision 64

6 Brontë, Lawrence and the 'Carbon' 78

7 Lawrence and the Counter-Culture 96

Coda 105

Bibliography 107

Index 113

FOREWORD

Emily Brontë's *Wuthering Heights* has something of an enigmatic quality which is yet pronounced enough to stimulate fresh critical reflection on what has continued to fascinate as a sort of "maverick" fiction. The thesis Dr. Celly builds around it and Lawrence taken together is one such. In its own day and even later the novel was considered rather simplistically as a sombre romance of love and sorrow, with the stormy Heathcliff, a gipsy waif, for central figure and villain whose love for Catherine Earnshaw, the daughter of his foster father, provided the core of the plot. And the novel's oddness was apt to be viewed as a youthful assault offensive to the deeply entrenched moralistic sensibilities of the Victorian elite. Emily's family circumstances explained much. The three Brontë sisters were spinning out poetry and creative prose amid their bleak and meagre existence in the wild desolation of Yorkshire moors. Emily was thought of as a lonely mysterious soul, a rebellious spirit in a fragile frame. And not only *Wuthering Heights* but also the few lyrics she left behind sustain that image, no less. They sound her characteristic sturdy note of "No coward soul is mine . . ." like that of the old Stoic of her own poem, asking of life no more than just the courage to endure. One could even sense a touch of a metaphysical yearning in her defiance: "I'll walk but not in old heroic traces. And not in paths of high morality. I'll walk where my own nature would be leading me." Her fiction, as well as her lyrics, is committed to a totally independent and *exclusive* claim to a spiritual experience.

All this notwithstanding, a serious and adequate assessment of her tale of bodily passion pursuing what seemed its *brute* loyalty beyond the barrier of death was hard to come by. Could there be some vital principle involved and affirmed in such an artistic demonstration discrediting, and indeed, in defiance of common moral norms? At best what critical reflection could suggest was that the novel helps reveal "a conscious paganism and pantheistic intuitions arraigned against the combined tyranny of society, family and religion" (Legouis and Cazamian). But the significance of Emily's fantastic dreams remained elusive. And the figures she had fashioned retained a curiously convincing yet unfathomable truth of their own. The issue remained open to fresh investigation in the light of modern and post-modern thinking.

The credit must go to Dr. Celly for having boldly assayed out to tackle this question. Using this unresolved issue as a jumping off plank he has broadened the scope of his thesis to what is seen as the European protest against a civilization that exalts the spirit and degrades the body—as he puts it. As supportive evidence he links the Emily Brontë novel with another well-known adversarial stance—that of D. H. Lawrence—Emily Brontë being "pre-eminently Lawrence's literary predecessor". What is common between them is that they form part of a European stream of protest against Western civilization. Lawrence had said, "With the coming of Socrates and the 'spirit' the cosmos died". And as the argument goes, the two dominant traditions of the West—the Socratic and the Christian—have instilled a distrust of the body, repudiating the passional and the instinctual life of man. Such a "betrayal" has been traumatic for the Western psyche causing pathological behaviours witnessed in the savagery of the World Wars, and the sado-masochistic elements in Western life generally.

The inevitable protest all this gave rise to was also central to the philosophical thought of thinkers like Rousseau, Nietzsche, and Freud. And the novels of Emily Brontë and Lawrence could be easily recognized to be its literary counter-part. They affirm their strong sense of the self rooted in the body; and their hostility towards Western civilization stems from the realization that it *negates* the self. Consequently, Dr. Celly points out, *Wuthering Heights* could be read not merely as a dramatization of the nature of passion; it could also be read as a demonstration that the Christian ethic and the Christian myth of Heaven are a negation of *being*. And that Lawrence, on his part, rejects the entire Platonic-Christian adventure called Western civilization as it bullies the body and alienates man from the non-human world. In offering an alternative, Dr. Celly takes the stand that the human self is not to be equated with the "ego", that life is prior to and larger than will or mentality.

Admittedly, the entity we call "self" and its possible transformations articulated in fictional terms in the case of Lawrence's Ursula needed elaboration somewhat. The author, however, seems to have thought, that would exceed the scope of his thesis. As it is, he has pursued the main thrust of his thesis—namely, neglect and degradation of the physical bodily experience, the life of passions and instinctual life—linking his literary critical interest in Emily Brontë and Lawrence to the profound disillusionment with Western civilization's monumental successes that has emerged in modern and post-modern thinking. It was pertinent to ask: How far do such present-day movements of thought reflect or, may be, corroborate the arraignment of civilization implicit in recent fiction?

For this purpose, Dr. Celly has brought within the scope of discussion, in support of his thesis, two dynamic figures who loom on the intellectual horizon today. One is Theodore Roszak of the "counter-culture" fame whose sustained exposure of the current obsession with "head-trips" so integral to the contemporary mental climate, and consequences of modern man's loss of a sense of transcendence have made an impression. And the other, Norman Brown whose book *Life Against Death,* particularly its last chapter captioned "The Resurrection of the Body", directly bears upon the present theme. Both these thinkers that Dr. Celly has cited add substance and, directly or indirectly, help vindicate his stand.

One last word: I imagine, for those of an Indian cast of mind there is nothing here, in this plea for "the resurrection of the body", that would be inherently unacceptable. Lacking anything like a sense of the sinfulness of the body *per se.* (After all, it is *prakriti, guna*-bound.) They can respect its nature, claims and rights without inhibition. So that the poet Yeats's words affirming art's commitment to the body might eminently serve as message or motto for this study:

> Art bids us touch and taste, and hear and see the world and shrink from what Blake called the mathematical form, from all that abstract thing, from all that is of the brain only and not a jetting forth from the entire hopes, memories, and sensations of the body. . . .
>
> —"The Thinking of the Body"

And we may recall that, of the English poets, Yeats's Indian experience was one of the most authentic.

Baroda V.Y. KANTAK

PREFACE

This book has taken a long time indeed. It had its origin nearly thirty years back in somewhat mundane circumstances when I was asked to 'do' *Wuthering Heights* with first year Honours students. As my luck would have it, they turned out to be a very bright lot and, what is more, very inquisitive. A lively dialogue followed making it all a very heady experience.

From then on reading *Wuthering Heights* and talking about it with colleagues and students has been a great joy of my life. Here was, it seemed to me, a literary text whose appeal was not narrowly aesthetic or even intellectual. It seemed to hit me in the middle of my being. Like Catherine Earnshaw's dream, it had gone through me "like wine through water and altered the colour of my mind".

At a certain point of time, the desire to articulate my response in writing became very strong. And then a friend of mine introduced me to Professor Kantak—he has graciously agreed to write a foreword too—that doyen among English teachers who has spent a lifetime shaping young academics rather than just writing books. When I discussed with Professor Kantak my 'thesis' on Brontë, he showed keen interest and suggested I could profitably read Lawrence's novels along with *Wuthering Heights.* Professor Kantak's suggestion turned out to be a brilliant one, for the affinities between the two novelists are striking indeed. I was also surprised by the fact that very little critical notice had been taken of them.

Brontë and Lawrence struck me as gorgeous yea-sayers and their works the grand affirmation of life. No wonder, they quarrelled with civilization they were born in. Reading their works was at once an exhilarating and a liberating experience somewhat comparable to what Will undergoes when he marries Ann in *The Rainbow.* The "tablets of stone" simply went bounding down the hill. To say more would be to anticipate. Let the book speak for itself.

Admittedly, it isn't fashionable to talk about literature in such naive, enthusiastic terms. Criticism is supposed to be objective and dispassionate. I believe, however, that knowledge, in humanities at any rate, cannot be exclusively cerebral; it must be holistic. Knowledge divorced from human emotions is an alienated activity, or worse, just a peddling of academic goods for going up the professional ladder. Affectless cognition may be the distinction of a robot, not of a human being. As Rousseau put it, "Why should a man exempt from desires and fears want to know?"

It would be only appropriate to end this brief preface with a reference to Lawrence's poem 'Thought':

> Thought it not a trick, or an exercise, or a set of dodges,
> Thought is a man in his wholeness wholly attending.

ACKNOWLEDGEMENTS

I am grateful to Professor R. K. Kaul, Professor Amritjit Singh, Professor V. N. Arora, Professor Rajiv Verma and Dr. R. M. Pal for going through my work and offering useful suggestions.

I am equally thankful to my friends R. K. Agnihotri, A. L. Khanna, Anand Bhalla, S. C. Narula, Anil Bhatt, Dilip Basu and K. G. Varma for their valuable assistance, academic and otherwise. Special thanks are due to Dr. Rajend Mesthrie for tracking down some of the more difficult references.

Also, I am deeply indebted to Mr. Man Mohan Diwaker who taught me English in school and from whom I imbibed my love of literature.

Last but not the least, I would like to thank my wife Aruna and son Sumit whose emotional support enabled me to complete and publish this work.

ACKNOWLEDGEMENTS

Now, when the charioteer beholds the vision, and his whole soul warmed, and is full of the prickings and ticklings of desire. . . . Then the charioteer is worse off than ever; he falls back like a racer at the barrier, and with a still more violent wrench drags the bit out of the teeth of the wild steed, and covers his abusive tongue and jaws with blood, and forces his legs and haunches to the ground and punishes him sorely.

PLATO, *Phaedrus*

'Don't you think it's rather cruel, the way Socrates drives his black horse—jerking him till his mouth and tongue are full of blood, and bruising his haunches? . . . Either the black horse has a perfect right to his own existence and his own desires and gratifications, or he shouldn't exist. . . .'

LAWRENCE, *The First Lady Chatterley*

'. . . I *am* Heathcliff. . . .'

EMILY BRONTË, *Wuthering Heights*

Chapter 1

THROUGH THE MAZE OF CRITICISM

IT IS RATHER surprising that no comparative study of Emily Brontë and D. H. Lawrence exists to date.[1] Perhaps there is not even an article on the affinities—structural or thematic—between the two novelists, apart from some stray remarks by Mark Kinkead-Weekes and Keith Sagar that shall be discussed a little later. Hence one is left with no option other than dealing with critical opinions on the two novelists separately. However this is not meant to be an exhaustive survey. I shall restrict myself to a consideration of some significant critical opinions having a bearing on the critique of civilization from a vitalistic view-point. The term vitalistic is not being used in the philosophical sense here. It shall simply be taken to mean the quality of being intensely alive to the passional and/or the non-human dimension of human existence.

Broadly speaking, there are two ways of looking at *Wuthering Heights*—one, the 'metaphysical' or mystical way represented by David Cecil, Richard Chase and J. Hillis Miller; two, the Marxist/humanist represented most notably by Arnold Kettle and Q. D. Leavis.

It may seem odd to lump David Cecil, J. H. Miller and Richard Chase under the same caption, but they have one thing in common: they are united by their emphasis on the ideal, the transcendental. Thus, though Cecil rightly identifies the dialectical structure of the novel and was the first critic to appreciate the role that nature plays in *Wuthering Heights*, he places a singular emphasis on ultimate, cosmic principles. Discussing the "main features" of Brontë's "philosophy" Cecil observes:

> The first is that the whole created cosmos, animate and inanimate, mental and physical alike, is the expression of certain living spiritual principles—on the one hand what may be called the principle of

> storm—of the harsh, the ruthless, the wild, the dynamic, and on the other the principle of calm—of the gentle, the merciful, the passive and the tame.
>
> Secondly, in spite of their apparent opposition these principles are not conflicting. Either—Emily Brontë does not make clear which she thinks—each is the expression of a different aspect of a single pervading spirit; or they are the component parts of harmony. . . . The world of our experience is, on *the face of it*, full of discord. But that is only because in the cramped condition of their *earthly incarnation* these principles are directed from following the course that their nature dictates. . . . But when they are free from *fleshly bonds* they flow unimpeded and unconflicting; and even in this world their discords are transitory. The single principle that *ultimately* directs them sooner or later imposes an equilibrium (emphasis added).[2]

Cecil is inclined to take a mystical view of the novel and plays down the antagonism between two modes of consciousness—modes that he himself characterizes as those of calm and storm. Notice his use of phrases like "apparent opposition", "earthly incarnation" and "ultimately" etc.

J. Hillis Miller approaches Brontë from a "theological perspective" because in "De Quincey, Emily Brontë, Arnold and Hopkins theological perspective is most important and determines everything else".[3] Later in the chapter on E. Brontë Miller observes:

> It was perhaps Aunt Branwell who most directly imposed on the Brontë children notions which might have been held at that time either by a Methodist or by an Anglican influenced by Evangelicalism—the concept of the natural depravity of man, the need for a saving relation to God, the relative unimportance of systematic theology, and the insistence on a few simple ideas, such as the view that all pleasure is evil, the notion that all life here must be directed to the ultimate end of salvation, and the idea that only a life of restraint, abnegation and submission to duty will have any chance of reaching that end.[4]

I propose to show that *Wuthering Heights* repudiates the Protestant values that Miller attributes to her aunt's influence and in fact through the titanic figures of Catherine and Heathcliff affirms joy, pride and love of the earth.

Richard Chase conceives of a mission for the Brontë heroine

à la Toynbee and finds faults with her for not fulfilling it:

> The human protagonist of the cultural tragedy (Toynbee follows the theme of Goethe's Faust) must perform a dynamic act, which will set God and the Devil at war. In the path of the culture-hero there stands an obstacle. The dynamic act of the hero hurls him against the Obstacle—if he is overcome by it, the Devil has won the wager and society fails to advance along the path of civilisation; but if he overcomes it, God has won. . . . Our Brontë culture-heroine, then, is the human protagonist of the cosmic drama. Rochester and Heathcliff are portrayed as being at once God-like and Satanic. . . . The Brontë heroines fail in their mission; they refuse to venture so much; they will not accept the challenge of the God-Devil, for fear the Devil should win.[5]

In the first place, the bracketting of Rochester and Heathcliff does not make for critical understanding. Two, Catherine is too autonomous a person to be a missionary. In fact, the drama of *Wuthering Heights* is too passionate, too existential to lend itself to mystical (Cecil), theological (Miller) or anthropological interpretations.

The Marxist/Humanist critic approaches Emily Brontë's novel from a radically different perspective—an anthropocentric one which has little use for the elements and animals and hence can hardly do justice to the non-human dimension. For example, Arnold Kettle observes:

> *Wuthering Heights* is about England in 1847. The people it reveals live not in a never-never land but in Yorkshire. Heathcliff was born not in the pages of Byron, but in a Liverpool slum. The language of Nelly, Joseph and Hereton is the language of Yorkshire people. The story of *Wuthering Heights* is concerned not with love in the abstract but with the passions of living people, with property-ownership, the attraction of social comforts, the arrangement of marriages, the importance of education, the validity of religion, the relation of rich and poor.[6]

Similarly, Q. D. Leavis in "A Fresh Approach to *Wuthering Heights*" makes a "plea for criticism of *Wuthering Heights* to turn its attention to the human core of the novel, to recognise its truly human centrality".[7] Her "human centrality" betrays a singular deafness to the non-human strain in the Brontë music:

> But the whole episode of Hareton's birth and childhood exposes Catherine's insensibility that her *self-centered nature is essentially loveless.*

> He only reference to her own pregnancy later is the hope that a son's birth will 'erase Isabella's title to be Edgar's heir'[8] (emphasis added).

and,

> . . . a real flaw, however, is wholly inadequate illustration of the shared life and interests of himself (Heathcliff) and Catherine that makes it possible that on his return she should be so absorbed in conversing with him as to cut out immediately and altogether her young husband. After all, we reflect, they couldn't always have been talking about their childhood escapades—that it to say, we recognise a failure in creative interests here in the novelist, nor do we ever hear what they talk about till Catherine attacks him over Isabella and they quarrel, when it becomes clear to Catherine that *he can be only the monster he has been made by his history* (emphasis added).[9]

Thus, Q. D. Leavis reveals a pronounced bias against the chief protagonists of the drama: for her the important thing about Catherine is her "loveless", "self-centered" nature and Heathcliff is a "monster". Such moralistic zeal can hardly equip any one to appreciate the essentially Dionysian nature of the Catherine–Heathcliff relationship which is the core of Brontë's novel.

To sum up, it is my contention that neither the Marxist/humanist nor the metaphysical/mystical view can do justice to the uniqueness of the novel: the former because it shows no appreciation of its non-human dimension, the latter because it ignores its here-and-nowness—the flesh and blood quality of its protagonists. That no proper appreciation of *Wuthering Heights* is possible without taking into account the two should be obvious to anyone who comes to it without 'ideological' blinkers.

There is, however, the third approach to Brontë to which I subscribe. We may call it the elemental or vitalistic approach for it shows an awareness of the passional and/or the non-human. For the elemental or vitalistic critic too the novel has a dialectical structure but the polarity for him is a tangible reality not conveyed by 'cosmic' terms like calm and storm. It is a nature-culture polarity. And contrary to the popular notion, this way of looking at the novel appears as early as 1850. Sidney Dobell wrote what is considered to be the first perceptive review of the novel:

> That Catherine Earnshaw—at once so wonderfully fresh, so fearfully natural—new, 'as if brought from other spheres' and familiar as the recollection of some woeful experience—what can surpass the strange compatibility of her simultaneous loves; the involuntary art with which her two natures are so made to coexist, that in the very arms of her lover we dare not doubt her purity; the inevitable belief with which we watch the oscillations of the old and new elements in her mind, and the exquisite truth of the last victory of nature over education . . . ?[10]

Dobell shows a better understanding of Catherine's "two natures" than Arnold Kettle and Q. D. Leavis. Also, he identifies an important theme of the novel when he talks of "the exquisite truth of the last victory of nature over education". F. A. Bullock, in his Brontë Society address, argues on similar lines when he observes, "In her book you have it all—the cry for integration and wholeness. Humanity dies without nature, evil and unsatisfied, without humanity."[11]

In our times, Dorothy Van Ghent's essay on *Wuthering Heights* is perhaps the most comprehensive statement of nature-culture polarity:

> Essentially, *Wuthering Heights* exists for the mind as a tension between two kinds of reality: the raw, inhuman reality of anonymous natural energies, and the restrictive reality of civilized habits, manners and codes. The first kind of reality is given to the imagination in the violent figures of Catherine and Heathcliff, portions of the flux of nature, children of rock and heath and tempest, striving to identify themselves as human but disrupting all around them with their monstrous appetite for an inhuman kind of intercourse, and finally disintegrated from within by the very energies out of which they are made. . . . set over against the wilderness of inhuman reality is the quietly secular, voluntarily limited, safely human reality that we find in the gossipy concourse of Nelly Dean and Lockwood. . . . This second kind of reality is given also in the romance of Cathy and Hareton, where book learning and gentle manners and domestic charities form a little island of complacence.[12]

Dorothy Van Ghent tends to take a very 'romantic' view of the destruction of Catherine and Heathcliff. In my opinion, what destroys the two protagonists is not "the very energies out of which they are made" but their thwarting by a repressive civilization. Julian Moynahan's essay, "Pastoralism as Culture and Counter-Culture" provides the necessary corrective to Dorothy Van Ghent's romantic interpretation:

> It is, like the greatest English romantic art, about the renaturing of society without the destruction of society, or alternatively, about the realigning of society with the realm of wild nature. This process is rather appalling from society's ordinary point of view—say from the viewpoint of a Lockwood—but it is absolutely necessary to accomplish because it is of the nature of society, through its genius for abstracted forms, to withdraw from the matrix of nature into an etiolated condition of separateness.[13]

My focus on Brontë is a little different. I maintain that Brontë's work forms part of a protest against the idealistic civilization of the west—a civilization that repressed the body, equated salvation with self-immolation and viewed with horror the assertion of the human spirit. In this she belongs to the company of Rousseau, Nietzsche and D. H. Lawrence. Also, her deep sense of the non-human in human—her awareness that men and women are primal forces before they are social beings—makes her a precursor of Lawrence even more than Hardy.

* * *

If the sense of the non-human in human is the distinguishing feature of Lawrence's œuvre, F. R. Leavis' attempt to place him in "the great tradition" of Jane Austen, George Eliot, Joseph Conrad and Henry James is a little intriguing. For writers like Jane Austen and Henry James are the finest products of civilized consciousness and uphold 'civilized values' like urbanity, irony and detachment—values one hardly associates with Lawrence.

Also, I find Leavis' emphasis on "our own phase" and "twentieth century England"[14] somewhat misleading, for Lawrence is concerned not merely with the modern, industrial phase of Western civilization but the Platonic–Christian legacy in its entirety, that is, the legacy that makes man the measure of all things and gives reason the pride of place in human existence. Phrases like "twentieth century England" and "industrial civilization" recur in Laurentian criticism with a sickening regularity, ever since Leavis declared that Lawrence was the great writer of our own phase of civilization.[15]

I propose to show that Lawrence is a critic not only of Western civilization in its modern, industrial phase but of the whole enterprise in the three thousand years of its existence—the Platonic–Christian consciousness in its entirety. Keith Sagar seems to grasp the significance of Lawrence's achievement better when he describes Lawrence's works as "metaphors for revolt" against "his mother and Eastwood and England and ultimately the basic values of Western civilization".[16] In an earlier book on Lawrence, Sagar places him in a "much larger, two-thousand rather than two-hundred-year-old tradition." Sagar thus provides the necessary corrective to Leavis' somewhat curious placing in the "great" tradition:

> In such contexts as 'the Scott tradition that imposed on the novelist a romantic resolution of his themes' or even 'the tradition coming down from the eighteenth century that demanded a plane-mirror reflection of the surface of 'real' life, Dr. Leavis seems to me to be using the word 'tradition' in a sense which comes perilously close to the word 'convention'. I want to approach Lawrence as uncompromisingly unconventional and taking his place in a much larger, two-thousand rather than two-hundred-year-old tradition. . . . The tradition in which Lawrence virtually places himself in the 'Study of Thomas Hardy' is much nearer to this than to Leavis' great tradition: he shares with Sophoales, Shakespeare, Tolstoy and Hardy the quality of 'setting behind the small action of the protagonists the terrific action of unfathomed nature.'[17]

Another work which is of special relevance to our study is Eugene Goodheart's *The Utopian Vision of D. H. Lawrence.* This work sees Lawrence in a wider European intellectual "tradition" and underlines the radical nature of Lawrence's vision. I suppose it is this radicalism which Eliot found distasteful:

> His achievement has analogues in the history of literature—the achievement of Rousseau, Blake, Dostoevskay, Nietzsche, Rilke—but these analogues do not constitute a tradition in the meaning that usually attaches to the word. Continuity with the past, the handing-down of inherited cultural attitudes—tradition in this sense does not figure in Lawrence. He is rather, in the phrase of Nietzsche, one of 'the table-breakers' who appear at significant crises in culture and whose characteristic impulse is to divert the current of tradition into new and hitherto unknown channels. Lawrence and the other table-breakers were men

> possessed with a prophetic vision, for them the past was interesting only for those moments that prefigured the future.[18]

In an unpublished thesis, Dennis De Nitto comes to the interesting conclusion that Lawrence is a "primitivist". Employing Nietzsche's celebrated distinction between the Dionysian and the Apollonian, De Nitto suggests "a writer is a primitivist or utilises the approach of primitive vision when, convinced his age is predominantly Apollonian, he attempts to discover among more 'primitive' groups or individuals attitudes, beliefs and action that are capable of being reinterpreted and incorporated into his civilization."[19] However, De Nitto does not show enough appreciation of the radicalism of Lawrence's œuvre. A work that deals with nature-culture polarity in Lawrence is A. Burns' book *Nature and Culture in D. H. Lawrence.* Burns makes some perceptive remarks on Lawrence's affinities with Nietzsche and his differences with existentialists like Sartre. Particularly illuminating is his thesis connecting concepts of the self and the mechanical and organic principles. "The substitution of the mechanical for the organic principle is a new form of the dichotomy between the chosen self and the natural self."[20] However, he comes to a tame and rather innocuous conclusion when he observes that "In *Women in Love* the social and the natural self are examined in what Lawrence has now come to see as the most important places; in society itself—Shortlands and Breadalby—in art and culture and in human language. Each, so long as its horizons are closed, is seen as an unhealthy habitat for the self."[21] Lawrence's quarrel with art, as I hope to show, is a part of his general critique of humanistic presumption to be gods of the show as seen in Gudrun and Loerke in *Women in Love.*

Briefly, I would like to argue that Lawrence's novels indict not only modern, industrial civilization but also Western civilization in its entirety; also, they offer a non-humanist alternative to the anthropocentric-rationalistic civilization of the west in that it rests on wholeness of being and a living relationship with the universe. Moreover, in this he anticipates contemporary thinkers like Norman O. Brown and Theodore Roszak.

❋ ❋ ❋

As I stated in the very beginning, there is no comparative study of Emily Brontë and D. H. Lawrence—only some observations of a comparative nature by Keith Sagar and Mark Kinkead-Weekes. Sagar in his book *The Art of D. H. Lawrence* put his finger on a basic affinity between the two novelists. "Emily Brontë and Lawrence both care less about analysing what a woman feels than about grasping what she is".[22] In an essay written later "The Originality of *Wuthering Heights*" Sagar is even more forthright in affirming Lawrence's debt to Brontë and thus totally breaks away from the line taken by F. R. Leavis:

> In any case, it is not true that *Wuthering Heights* in a sport, only that it belongs to a much older and much less limiting tradition than that of the English realistic novel of the late 18th and 19th centuries. Behind her is certainly Shakespeare—what novel is closer to *Macbeth* or *King Lear*? Ahead of her is *The Heart of Darkness, The Rainbow, Women in Love, St Mawr*. She opened the way for developments in the novel which Lawrence was able to exploit only when he had weaned himself of the influence of George Eliot.[23]

Mark Kinkead-Weekes too makes some very perceptive remarks on the treatment of love in E. Brontë and Lawrence. Especially significant is Kinkead-Weekes' emphasis on impersonality in the two novelists:

> Though Emily Brontë is reticent, I should be inclined to say that all the love relationships in the novel are sexual. Only, the nature of sexuality differs as radically between the Grange and the Heights as everything else does. With Catherine and Heathcliff it seems to have nothing to do with sexual attraction and physical desire as such. Like all other aspects of their love, it seems to be concerned with a breaking through beyond the self metaphysical and impersonal as (in Lawrence whom this side of the novel often anticipates).[24]

While both Sagar and Kinkead-Weekes have greatly helped my understanding of the two novelists, I do have a feeling that neither of them has been able to free himself altogether from the 'metaphysical' legacy, for they both tend to play down the rich sense of the physical, of the body in Emily Brontë. Thus, Sagar remarks:

> There is no reverence for the life of the body as such in Emily Brontë. Rather the body is thought of as the prison-house of the tortured soul which can only find its fulfilment when totally unrestrained by limitations of any kind, social, moral or physical.[25]

Similarly, Kinkead-Weekes observes:

> If we do compare them (Catherine and Heathcliff) with Lawrence, there is neither the rich reverence for life through the body enhancing the whole relationship of man to the physical universe, not the concern for independent selfhood enriching relationship; which together make his kind of 'impersonality' so unsolipsistic.[26]

Emily Brontë may not have Lawrence's "reverence" but she does show a keen sense of life of the body—its wonder and mystery. It is present all through, in the "moorish and wild and knotty" quality of the novel (as Charlotte Brontë noted in her 1850 preface), in the relationship of Catherine and Heathcliff, in Catherine's awareness of the antagonism between *Wuthering Heights* and the Earth on the one hand and the Grange and Heaven on the other, in Heathcliff's indifference to the conventional heaven when he has attained his own, and, also in the predominance of elemental and animal imagery.

To anticipate briefly, this study attempts to do the following:

I. It sees both Lawrence and Brontë as part of a European stream of protest against a civilization that represses the body and thus perpetuates the mind-body dichotomy. It thus attempts to rescue the intellectual élan of Emily Brontë's classic that has been obscured by her reputation as a mystic (Chapter 2).

II. *Wuthering Heights* celebrates the a-moral magnificance and splendour of passion—a celebration which also serves as a focus on the inadequacy of civilized, Christian values like duty and humanity, the parental sentiment and above all the Christian myth of heaven. Also, the 'uncivilized' ones like Catherine and Heathcliff lead a rich psychic life in that their erotic and aggressive instincts are not thwarted. Emily Brontë may be called a primitivist in that sense (Chapter 3).

III. Lawrence is not only a critic of the modern, industrial civilization of the West but of its entire Platonic-Christian heritage—a fact which is not often appreciated. This essay attempts to establish this with reference to *The Rainbow,* "St. Mawr", *Lady Chatterly's Lover* and *Women in Love.* The last is seen to be Lawrence's most central statement on the subject (Chapter 4).

IV. Lawrence is not just a writer of wasteland novels. His work offers a nonrepressive alternative to the Western *cul de sac.* The alternative vision is rooted in an unself-conscious acceptance of the erotic and aggressive instincts and a living awareness of the non-human universe. This proposition is examined with particular reference to *Women in Love, Lady Chatterly's Lover,* "St. Mawr" and a short story called "Sun" (Chapter 5).

V. Emily Brontë is the precursor of D. H. Lawrence and the carbon metaphor that Lawrence employs to describe his fiction applies equally to *Wuthering Heights.* The rejection of the bourgeois novel with its manners-and-morals straitjacket is vitally related to their rejection of Western idealism and their perception that life is anterior to mentality (Chapter 6).

VI. Lawrence's position stands fully vindicated by what has comes to be known as counter-culture of the West. He seems to have striking affinities with thinkers like Norman O. Brown and Theodore Roszak, and may be rightly regarded as their precursor (Chapter 7).

NOTES AND REFERENCES

1. *D. H. Lawrence and Tradition* edited by Jeffrey Meyers (London: Athlone Press, 1985) has seven chapters dealing with Lawrence's relationship with Blake, Carlyle, Ruskin, George Eliot, Hardy, Whitman and Nietzsche but none on Emily Brontë. Apparently, Brontë is not considered one of the 'most dominant influences' on Lawrence.
2. "Emily Brontë and Wuthering Heights", *Emily Brontë: Penguin Critical Anthologies,* ed. Jean Pierre Petit (Harmondsworth: Penguin, 1923), p. 94.
3. *The Disappearance of God* (Cambridge: Harvard University Press, 1963), p. VIII.
4. Ibid., p. 181.
5. *The Brontës: Twentieth Century Views,* ed. Ian Gregor (New Jersey: Prentice Hall, 1970), p. 27.
6. *An Introduction to the English Novel* (1951; rpt London: Hutchinson University Library, 1965), p. 139.

7. F. R. & Q. D. Leavis, *Lectures in America* (London: Chatto and Windus, 1969), p. 137.
8. Ibid., p. 94.
9. Ibid., p. 96.
10. "Currer Bell", *Palladium* (Sept. 1850) quoted from *Emily Brontë: Penguin Critical Anthologies*, p. 38.
11. Quoted from Melvin Watson's "Wuthering Heights and the Critics", *Nineteenth Century Fiction*, 3 (1949), p. 257.
12. *Emily Brontë: Penguin Critical Anthologies*, p. 118.
13. "Pastoralism as Culture and Counter-Culture in English Fiction, 1800-1928", *Towards A Poetics of Fiction*, ed Mark Spilka (Bloominton and London: Indiana University Press, 1977), p. 247.
14. In her biography of Lawrence, Brenda Maddox observes that Frieda Lawrence "scolded" Leavis for "over-Englishing" Lawrence. "From *The Rainbow* on, she explained to Leavis (who had made a personal crusade of championing Lawrence's greatness), Lawrence is no longer a British writer but a universal one." *The Married Man—A Life of D. H. Lawrence* (London: Sinclair-Stevenson, 1994), p. 531.
15. "He is still the great writer of our own phase of civilization" and *Women in Love* "contains a presentation of twentieth century England, of modern civilization—so firsthand and searching in its comprehensiveness as to be beyond the power of any other novelist he (the reader) know of." *D. H. Lawrence: Novelist* (1955; rpt Penguin 1964), p. 178.
16. *The Life of D. H. Lawrence—An Illustrated Biography* (London: Eyre Methuen, 1980), p. 60.
17. *The Art of D. H. Lawrence* (Cambridge: Cambridge University Press, 1966), p. 5.
18. *The Utopian Vision of D. H. Lawrence* (Chicago: University of Chicago Press, 1963), p. 5.
19. *Modern Literary Primitivism in the Writings of D. H. Lawrence and other British Novelists*, unpublished Ph. D. Thesis, Columbia University, 1966.
20. *Nature and Culture in D. H. Lawrence* (London: Macmillan, 1980), p. 78.
21. Ibid., p. 113.
22. *The Art of D. H. Lawrence*, p. 44.
23. "The Originality of *Wuthering Heights*", *The Art of Emily Brontë*, ed. Anne Smith (London: Vision Press, 1976), p. 132.
24. "The Place of Love in *Jane Eyre* and *Wuthering Heights*", The Brontës: Twentieth Century Views, p. 88.
25. *The Art of Emily Brontë*, p. 151.
    I felt greatly assured by Lyn Pykett's observation that *Wuthering Herights* "looks forward to D. H. Lawrence's religion of the body . . ." *Emily Brontë* (London: Macmillan, 1989), p. 34.
26. *The Brontës: Twentieth Century Views*, pp. 93–94.

Chapter 2

BRONTË, LAWRENCE AND THE PROTEST AGAINST CIVILIZATION

IN MODERN TIMES the Western mind reveals a strong sense of disenchantment with its idealistic civilization. This is not necessarily a consequence of what is known as Decline of the West, for the note of protest is clearly heard as early as Rousseau who, both by his writings and his bohemian life-style, marks a definite shift in European sensibility. In Nietzsche, as later in Lawrence, Norman O. Brown and Theodore Roszak, we have an even more radical questioning of the norms and values by which the Western man has lived. Even Freud, notwithstanding the fact that he is a child of the Enlightenment, belongs to this 'protestant' stream, since "cultural privation" is a recurrent theme in his philosophical writings. It is proposed to show here that both Emily Brontë and Lawrence share significant intellectual concerns with Rousseau, Nietzsche, Freud and, in our times, with Norman O. Brown and Roszak.[1] What unites the philosophical writings of Rousseau and Freud with the novels of Lawrence and Emily Brontë is their strong sense of the self and the belief affirmed with varying degrees of emphasis that it is rooted in the body. Also, their dissatisfaction with Western civilization stems from the realization that it negates the self. In fact, the violence and destructiveness of Western civilization is seen by almost all of them to result from its denial of the body. Also, while no one exactly advocates a return to nature, not even Rousseau,[2] they may all be called primitivists in that they believe that primitive man was superior to 'civilized' man since he lived a richer psychic life.

Rousseau's works are marked by a profound concern with the self and the threats it faces from the prevailing social norms and values. Even in his early, somewhat amateurish, polemical *Discourse on the Arts and Sciences* that he wrote in 1750, he shows as awareness of the repressive nature of social norms; however, he posits too facile an antithesis between the advancement of arts and sciences and the moral health of a given society:

> We no longer dare seem what we really are, but lie under a perpetual restraint; in the meantime the herd of men, which we call society, all act under the same circumstances exactly alike, unless very particular and powerful motives prevent them. Thus we never know with whom we have to deal; and even to know our friends we must wait for some critical and pressing occasion.[3]

In Discourse on Inequality Rousseau pursues this theme much more seriously. He contrasts the savage with the citizen to make the point that the citizen's life is a falsity. ". . . the savage lives within himself, whereas the citizen, constantly besides himself, knows only how to live in the opinion of others, in so much that it is, if I may say so, merely from their judgement that he derives the consciousness of his own existence."[4]

In *Lettre D' Alembert* Rousseau denounces the French love of theatre as "extraneous amusement", rooted in self-evasion. "It is dissatisfaction with oneself, it is the burden of restlessness, it is the forgetting of simple and natural tastes, that makes necessary extraneous amusement."[5] Later, in the same *Lettre*, his appeal to his countrymen not to abandon their public festivals anticipates Lawrence's vision of Greater Society. "It is in the open air, under the sky, that you should come together and abandon yourselves to the sweet feelings of your happiness."[6]

Similarly, Rousseau attacks the contemporary system of education for its life-negating norms. "What is to be thought of that cruel education which sacrifices the present to an uncertain future, that burdens the child with all sorts of restrictions and begins by making him miserable, in order to prepare him for some far off happiness which he may never enjoy."[7] Particularly scathing is his criticism of "foresight"—the cornerstone of civilized existence—"which is ever begging us to look forward into the future, a future which in many cases we shall never reach."[8] Rousseau's perception of the civilized man's obsessive concern with the future as life-denying anticipates not only Nietzsche and Lawrence but also contemporary thinkers like Norman O. Brown and Theodore Roszak.

Above all, Rousseau is perhaps the first modern thinker to see that knowledge is rooted in human passions and is not a disembodied activity, and that the sensual and the spiritual must not be split and set against one another. In *Discourse on Inequality* he observes:

> Let moralists say what they will, the human understanding is greatly indebted to the passions, which, on their side, are likewise universally allowed to be greatly indebted to the human understanding. It is by the activity of our passions, that our reason improves. We covet knowledge merely because we covet enjoyment; it is impossible to conceive why a man exempt from fears and desires should take the trouble to reason.[9]

To declare that "a man exempt from fears and desires" will not "take the trouble to reason" is to affirm the union of the spiritual and the sensual, and to reject altogether the Platonic position as stated in *Phaedo* and summed up in the observation, "The Philosopher disrespects the body". It also anticipates the Freudian discovery that there is no such thing as pure contemplation.[10]

Nietzsche shows even a clearer perception of the unity of the sensual and the spiritual, and hence his forthright attack on Greek rationalism and Christian morality. He is perhaps the first thinker to offer a pathological perspective on Socratic commitment to reason. (Freud admired Nietzsche for the diagnostic insight his writings offered in Western culture.[11]) In "Twilight of the Idols" he observes:

> Socrates was a misunderstanding: the entire morality of improvement, the Christian included, has been a misunderstanding. . . . The harshest daylight, rationality at any cost, life bright, cold, circumspect, conscious, without instinct, in opposition to the instincts, has itself been no more than a form of sickness, another form of sickness—and by no means a way back to 'virtue', to 'health', to happiness . . . To have to combat one's instincts—that is the formula for *decadence*: as long as life is ascending, happiness and instinct are one.[12]

In Nietzsche's opinion the Socratic commitment to reason is pathological. Reason is being employed as a weapon, a "countertyrant" to combat the instincts. "The fanaticism with which the whole of Greek thought throws himself at rationality betrays a state of emergency. One was in peril, one has only one choice, either to perish or be absolutely rational."[13]

The Socratic commitment to reason may or may not be called "decadent", but it cannot be denied that the exaltation of reason is at the expense of instincts and is meant to combat them. That Plato-Socrates betrays a fear of the instincts is clearly borne out by the treatment of the black horse in *Phaedrus*:

> Now, when the charioteer beholds the vision, and his whole soul warmed through sense, and is full of the prickings and ticklings of desire. . . . Then the charioteer is worse off than ever; he falls back like a racer at the barrier, and with a still more violent wrench drags the bit out of the teeth of the wild steed, and covers his abusive tongue and jaws with blood, and forces his legs and haunches to the ground and punishes him sorely.[14]

The same fear of the body expresses itself in *Phaedo:*

> And thought is best when the mind is gathered into herself and none of these things trouble her—neither sounds nor sights nor pain nor any pleasure—when she takes leave of the body, and has as little as possible to do with it, when she has no bodily sense or desire, but is aspiring after true being? And in this the philosopher dishonours the body. . . .[15]

Thus Nietzsche's insight that the man who describes life as a prolonged illness must himself be sick is corroborated by the overall approach that Plato-Socrates shows towards the sensual self. To set reason against instincts is to perpetuate a division in the human psyche and thus become ill. No wonder, when he was about to die, Socrates felt that he owed a cock to Asculapius.

Nietzsche denounces Christian morality for much the same reason; it is repressive and deprives man of "joy" and "pride"—always terms of approbation in the Nietzschean lexicon as they are in Lawrence's. Christian morality tries to improve man by taming him, by draining him of all vitality. "In the early Middle Ages, when the Church was in fact above all a menagerie, one every where hunted down the fairest specimens of the 'blond beast'—one 'improved', for example, the noble Teutons. But what did such a Teuton afterwards look like when he had been 'improved' and led into a monastery like a caricature of a human being, like an abortion: he had become a 'sinner', he was in a cage, one had imprisoned him behind nothing but sheer terrifying concepts . . ."[16]

The means it employed to emasculate man were the twin concepts of sin and that of the Kingdom of God.[17] While the latter devalues life on this earth ("Life is at an end where the Kingdom of God begins")[18], the concept of sin with its concomitant guilt-and-punishment syndrome deprives him of all pride and joy, particularly the joy of the senses. "Hatred of *mind*, of pride, courage, freedom, *libertinage* of mind is Christian; hatred of the *senses*, of the joy of the senses, of joy in general is Christian. . . ."[19]

Thus, for Nietzsche, Christianity is the negation of all that constitutes health and well-being. At the root of Christian morality is the same fear of life as marked the Socratic commitment to reason. And he advocates liberation from the sick Christian heritage by linking the sense of guilt with the denial of instincts. "Man has far too long regarded his natural proclivities with an 'evil eye', so that eventually they have become in his system affiliated with a bad conscience. A converse endeavour would be intrinsically feasible . . . namely, to affiliate to the bad conscience all those unnatural proclivities. . . ."[20]

Owing to his unequivocal commitment to culture, Freud does not take as radical a position as Nietzsche. But he is equally aware of the sacrifice of "natural proclivities" that culture entails. In Freud's view the price exacted by culture in terms of individual instinctual fulfilment was very high, and seemed to threaten its very fabric. Man's hostility to culture is a recurrent theme in Freud's philosophical writings. In his essay, "The Most Prevalent Form of Degradation in Erotic Life" Freud observes:

> . . . altogether it is not possible for the claim of the sexual instinct to be reconciled with the demands of culture, that in consequence of his cultural development renunciation and suffering, as well as the danger of his extinction at some far future time are not to be eluded by the race of man.[21]

In *Thoughts for the Times on War and Death,* his observations amount to a virtual indictment of "civilized society". "Civilized society, which exacts good conduct does not trouble itself about the impulses underlying it, has thus won over to obedience a great many people who are not thereby following the dictates of their own natures. Encouraged by the success, society has suffered itself to be led into straining the moral standard to the highest possible point, and thus it has forced its members into a yet greater estrangement from their instinctual dispositions."[22]

However, Freud's most important exposition of the subject is to be found in *Civilization and Its Discontents.* It is remarkable that the great apologist of culture shows an acute awareness of "cultural privation"—the great price that individuals have to pay in terms of instinctual deprivation to build culture. ". . . it is impossible to ignore the extent to which civilization is built up on renunciation of instinctual gratification, the degree to which the existence of civilization presupposes the non-gratification (suppression, repression, or something else?) of powerful instinctual energies. This cultural privation dominates the whole field of social relations between human beings."[23]

Later, in the same essay, Freud concedes what is usually dismissed as a romantic myth, namely, the superiority of the primitive man. "If civilization requires such sacrifices not only of sexuality but also of the aggressive tendencies in mankind, we can better understand why it should be so hard for men to feel happy in it. In actual fact, primitive man was better off in this respect, for he knew nothing of any restrictions on his instincts."[24]

However, Freud considers "such sacrifices" of sexuality and aggression as a necessary condition of the power that civilization confers on man—the power to control natural forces and to regulate human relations. This makes Freud's attitude towards cultural imperatives somewhat ambivalent. Freud's discussion of the Christian commandment "Love Thy Neighbour"—the cornerstone of idealistic ethic—brings out this characteristic ambivalence:

> The command to love our neighbours as ourselves is the strongest defence there is against human aggressiveness and it is a superlative example of the unpsychological attitude of the cultural superego.[25]

Thus Freud describes the Christian commandment to love one's neighbour as "a superlative example of the unpsychological attitude of the superego" and yet endorses it as the "strongest defence there is against human aggressiveness." If the command to love one's neighbour is "completely at variance with original human nature", then it is unlikely to prove much of a defence against human aggressiveness. For in living by such an impossible precept, the human psyche is subjected to an extraordinary strain and is bound to revolt. The widespread violence of our times, particularly the two World Wars, provide ample testimony to this. For Freud "Love Thy Neighbour" is, to borrow Nietzsche's phrase, a sort of "countertyrant", and nobody was better equipped to know of its helplessness in the face of the unconscious than Freud himself. Norwithstanding its ambivalence, the essential thrust of his philosophical writings is radical as it recognizes the power of the passional self. Alfred Kazin offers a brilliant summing up of Freud's achievement in the essay "The Freudian Revolution Analysed":

> What Freud proclaimed above all else was that 'nature' which is nearest to us in the erotic side of man, and which culture and society are always pushing away as unworthy of man's 'higher' nature, has constantly to be brought back into man's awareness. Freud saw in man's sexual instinct a force of profound natural urgency, a whole system of energies, which could be repressed and forgotten and pushed back into the unconsciousness only at the cost of unnecessary strain and even of self-destructiveness. . . . Civilization, as we know it, Freud said, had been built up on man's heroic sacrifice of instinct. Only, Freud issued the warning that more and more men would resent this sacrifice, would wonder if civilization was worth the price.[26]

* * *

On a superficial view, it may appear odd to place Emily Brontë in the company of Rousseau, Nietzsche, Freud and even Lawrence. While the greatness of her work has been appreciated, its intellectual vigour has not received adequate attention. The Brontë legend seems to have obscured the intellectual élan of her work. However Charlotte Brontë seemed to appreciate this aspect of her sister's genius when she wrote:

> In some points I consider Ellis somewhat of a theorist. Now and then he broaches ideas which strike my sense as much more daring and original than practical, his reason may be in advance of mine, but certainly it often travels a different road. . . .[27]

Admittedly, Brontë is no 'thinker' as Nietzsche is and, unlike Lawrence, she is the sort of writer deriving ideas from whose work could be a hazardous enterprise. Still one could safely aver that her masterpiece *Wuthering Heights* subjects the basic norms and values of Western civilization to the most ruthless scrutiny, something that one associates with Nietzsche.[28] Nor is this a gratuitous comparison. Compare, for instance, Nietzsche's evaluation of categorical imperatives in *The Genealogy of Morals* with Heathcliff's contemptuous dismissal of "duty" and "humanity" in *Wuthering Heights*:

> I believe that everything which we Europeans of today are in the habit of admiring as the values of all these things called 'humanity', 'mankind', 'sympathy', 'pity', may be of some value as the debilitation and moderating of certain powerful and dangerous primitive impulses. Nevertheless, in the long run all these things are nothing else than the belittlement of the entire type 'man', his mediocrisation. . . .[29]

and,

> 'That is quite possible', remarked Heathcliff, forcing himself to seem calm, 'quite possible that your master should have nothing but common humanity and a sense of duty to fall back upon . . . ? (*Wuthering Heights*, p. 185)[30]

Nietzsche concedes that the civilized values are useful, but they *belittle* (emphasis added) the entire type of man. Heathcliff's retort to Nelly implies that Edgar's "duty" and "humanity" are poor substitutes for the primitive passion he (Heathcliff) offers—"something to fall back upon". In Nietzschean terms, Edgar is a mediocre compared to Heathcliff. It might be suggested that Heathcliff is only one character in the novel and to equate him with the writer is hardly proper. But the insight into the inadequacy of values like 'pity' and 'sympathy' is a part of the total vision as I hope to show in the next chapter.

Again, Brontë sees both the Christian ethic of forgiveness and the Christian concept of heaven as negation of self. Heathcliff rejects Nelly Dean's exhortation to forgive Hindley as it leaves 'I' out of account altogether, "God won't have the satisfaction that I shall" (p. 101). That Heathcliff's reaction is normal, not an aberration, is established by the similar reaction of Isabella vis-a-vis Heathcliff. "But what misery laid on Heathcliff would content me, unless I have a hand in it?" (p. 215). Earlier in the novel, Jabes Branderham's conduct in Lockwood's dream provides an implicit indictment of Christian ethic. The doctrine of infinite forgiveness, here exemplified in the sermon "Seventy-times Seven", is bound to degenerate into absurd literalism as witnessed in Branderham's conduct and that of the entire assembly with the result that "everyman's hand is against his neighbour". The doctrine of infinite forgiveness is, to borrow Freud's phrase, "a superlative example of the unpsychological attitude of the superego" and only serves to suppress and then explode the dammed up violence.

An allied theme in Emily Brontë is cruelty of the civilized. Cruelty of the civilized is a measure of the inadequacy of civilization, of its inability to contain or educate destructive emotions. While the 'uncivilized' like Heathcliff and Catherine own their destructive impulses and live them out, they find devious expression in the lives of the 'civilized'. Thus, Lockwood rubs the wrist of the child on a windowpane. Isabella sees Heathcliff hang her dog and Edgar Linton shuts himself up in his books when his wife is dying.

Above all, Emily Brontë—at any rate the Emily Brontë of *Wuthering Heights*—seems to see the Christian concept of heaven as negation of being, Catherine's revelation of her dream of Nelly amounts to the rejection of heaven as the realm of not-being. ". . . heaven did not seem to be my home; and I broke my heart with weeping to come back to earth; and the angels were so angry that they flung me out, into the middle of the heath on the top of Wuthering Heights, where I woke sobbing for joy . . ." (p. 121). The angels recognize the blasphemous nature of Catherine's desire, and angrily fling her down. She is filled with joy to see herself back on earth. Heathcliff rejects the Christian heaven even more emphatically telling Nelly, ". . . I have nearly attained my heaven; and that of others is altogether unvalued, and uncoveted by me!" (p. 363). In their joyous affirmation of life on earth, and rejection of heaven as the realm of alienation, the Brontë protagonists remind one of Nietzsche's observation, "The saint in whom God takes pleasure is the ideal castrate. Life is at end when the 'kingdom of God' begins."[31] Even more, Lawrence's magnificent conclusion to *Apocalypse.* "For man, the vast marvel is to be alive. For man, as for flower and beast and bird, the supreme bird is to be most vividly, most perfectly alive. . . . The dead may look after the afterwards. But the magnificent here and now of life in the flesh is ours. . . ."[32]

Lawrence's affinities with Nietzsche are even more striking. There is the same love of the rolling phrase, the same propensity for the extremist statement. Their *bête noires* are the same—Socratism and Christianity; and "joy" and "pride" are terms of approbation with both. And the writings of both Nietzsche and Lawrence are marked by a tremendous spirit of exhilaration and freedom. What distinguishes Lawrence from Nietzsche, however, is the non-human dimension of his vision, the sense of the numinous, that saves him from the *cul de sac* of humanistic presumption which was Nietzsche's undoing.

Like Nietzsche, Lawrence too comes down heavily on Plato and Christianity for their denial of the body—"blood-consciousness" in Lawrence's phrase. In one of his most significant letters to Bertrand Russell written in 1915 Lawrence affirms, "I have been reading Frazer's *Golden Bough* and *Totemism and Exogamy.* Now I am convinced of what I believed when I was twenty—that there is another seat of consciousness than the brain and the nerve system: there is a blood-consciousness which exists in us independently of the ordinary mental consciousness. . . ."[33] In the same letter, he denounces both Russell and Plato for letting mental consciousness tyrannize over blood-consciousness:

> And the tragedy of this our life, and of your life, is that the mental and nerve consciousness exerts a tyranny over the blood-consciousness, and that your will has gone completely over to the mental-consciousness, and is engaged in the destruction of your blood-being or blood-consciousness, the final liberating of the one, which is only death in result. Plato was the same.[34]

Similarly, in a letter written to Catherine Carswell a few months later, Lawrence denounces Christianity as a negation. "Christianity is based on reaction, on negation really. It says, 'Renounce all worldly desires and live for heaven'. Whereas I think people ought to fulfil sacredly their desires."[35] Lawrence continued to see the Platonic-Christian idealism as the primary Western malady and the modern industrial civilization as the culmination of Western idealism. In *Apocalypse*, the last thing that Lawrence wrote, he holds to his diagnosis:

> Christianity and our ideal civilization have been one long evasion. It has caused endless lying and misery, misery such as people know today, not of physical want but of far more deadly want. Better lack bread than lack life. The long evasion, whose only fruit is the machine.[36]

A little later in the same book he observes:

> With the coming of Socrates and 'the spirit', the cosmos died. For two thousand years man has been living in a dying universe, hoping for a heaven hereafter. And all the religious have been religions of the dead body and the postponed reward: eschatological, to use a pet word of the philosophers.[37]

Also, in a letter to Trigant Burrow, Lawrence denounced the motto "man is the measure of the universe"—something which is central to both Plato and Christianity—as "the idiotic footrule".[38] Thus, Lawrence indicts the Platonic-Christian legacy on two counts: one, that it exalts the spirit over the body thus leading to the constant bullying of the passional self, and two, that it exalts man over the rest of creation and thus alienates him from it.

While Lawrence was no philosopher in the accepted sense of the term, his understanding of the Platonic-Christian legacy was essentially sound—something he had felt on his pulse. Thinkers like Ernst Cassirer, C. G. Jung and H. Richard Niebuhr have attested to its pronounced anthropocentric-rationalistic bias.

Niebuhr the Christian thinker for instance, admits in his book *Christ and Culture* that the Christian love of man is "pure Agape". "But the love of man is pitiful rather than adoring, it is giving and forgiving rather than grateful, it suffers for and in their seriousness and profaneness; it does not consent to accept them as they are but calls them to repentance."[39] In *The Man Who Died* Lawrence attacks Jesus Christ for the condescending and passionless love he offers men—Niebuhr's "pitiful love"—and it is this that Jesus discards in the Laurentian rendering of the Resurrection and wakes to the beauty of the phenomenal world.

In *An Essay on Man* Cassirer notes the anthropocentric shift that occurs in Greek philosophy with Socrates:

> But this new tendency of thought, although in a sense inherent in early

> Greek philosophy, did not come to its full maturity until the time of Socrates. Thus it is in the problem of man that we find the landmark separating Socratic from pre-Socratic thought.[40]

Similarly, Jung notes Christianity's "rigidly anthropomorphic view" and its disastrous consequences for Western man. In his essay "Role of the Unconscious" he observes:

> It is no accident that official Christianity has no relationship with the animal. This omission particularly, striking in comparison with Buddhism, is often felt by sensitive people and has moved one modern poet to sing of a Christ who sacrifices his life for the sufferings of dumb animals. . . . By being repressed into the unconscious, the source from which it originated, the animal in us only becomes more beastlike, and that is no doubt the reason why the world has never seen a bloodier war than the war of the Christian nations.[41]

Jung's diagnosis of the Western disease that it is the repression of the animal which is responsible for the murderous violence of Christian nations is strikingly close to Lawrence's. One particularly thinks of Rupert Birkin, a thinly veiled portrait of the author himself, in *Women in Love* and his observation: "But they maintain a lie, and so they run amok at last" (p. 141). Lawrence sees Western civilization as the Jesus-Judas syndrome: 'Jesus' is not always Jesus Christ, he is sometimes Plato. In either case, this civilization embodies the impossible idealism that has plagued the Western man and is seen as a lie making the revolt of the thwarted unconscious inevitable.[42] Lawrence's novels enact this Jesus-Judas syndrome or, to employ Plato's telling metaphor, they narrate the Western man's one-steed journey into consciousness and its consequences.

To sum up, Rousseau, Nietzsche, Freud, Emily Brontë and Lawrence are all united in their repudiation of Western idealism which exalts the spiritual over the physical and thus perpetuates spirit-body dichotomy. The integrity of the self is seen to be threatened by 'society' with its genius for abstraction and its obsession with foresight and future. Also, as the tendency to bully the body is by no means confined to Western civilization, their works provide an implicit critique of all civilizations which sacrifice present to future, spontaneity to foresight, and emotional fulfilment to intellectual achievement.

I shall now turn to the novels of Emily Brontë and Lawrence to examine how it (the critique) actually works in terms of narrative and enactment.

NOTES AND REFERENCES

1. Norman O. Brown and Theodore Roszak are dealt with in Ch.7 under the caption, "Lawrence and Counter-Culture".
2. Lovejoy in his essay "The Supposed Primitivism of Rousseau's *Discourse on Inequality*" tries to refute the notion that Rousseau is a primitivist. "The notion that Rousseau's *Discourse on Inequality* was essentially a glorification of the state of nature and that its influence tended wholly or chiefly to promote 'primitivism' is one of the most persistent of historical errors." *Modern Philology*, 21(1923–24), p. 165.

   It is true that Rousseau does not glorify the state of nature or advocate a return to it, but he does believe that the primitive man is happier than the civilized man for he leads a more authentic and more integrated existence.
3. *The Social Contract and Discourses*, trans. G.D.H. Cole (New York: E.P. Dulton & Co., 1950), p. 149.
4. *French and English Philosophers*, ed. Charles W. Eliot (Collier: Harvard Classics, 1938), xxxiv, p. 227.
5. *The Indispensable Rousseau*, Comp. John Hope Mason (London: Quartet Books, 1979), p. 123.
6. Ibid., p. 131.

   Even as hostile a critic as Irving Babbitt concedes that "Occidental man did not before Rousseau show much inclination to mingle with the landscape". *Rousseau and Romanticism*, (1919, rpt. Boston & New York: Houghton Mifflin Comp., 1968, p. 292).
7. Ibid., p. 187.
8. Ibid., p. 188.
9. *French and English Philosophers*, ed. Charles W. Eliot, p. 177.
10. Norman O. Brown observes in *Life Against Death*, "Freudian psychology eliminates the category of pure contemplation as non-existent" (New York: Random House, 1959), p. 8.
11. ". . . according to Ernest Jones, Freud's biographer, Freud 'several times said of Nietzsche that he had a more penetrating knowledge of himself than any other man who ever lived or was ever likely to live.' " Walter Kaufmann, 'Nietzsche', *Encyclopedia of Philosophy*, Vol V. ed-in-chief Paul Edwards (New York: Macmillan, 1967), p. 505.
12. *Twilight of the Idols and The Anti-Christ*, trans. R. J. Hollingdale (Harmondsworth: Penguin, 1968), p. 34.

13. Ibid., p. 33.
14. *Dialogues of Plato*, trans, Benjamin Jowett, 'Great Books of the Western World', ed-in-chief Robert M. Hutchins (Chicago: Encyclopedia Britannica 1952), p. 128.
15. Ibid., p. 224.
16. *Twilight of the Idols and The Anti-Christ*, p. 56.
17. Even F. Copleston, a Christian thinker, admits that "the Christian conception of God does involve the belief that this life is not the only life nor even the richest life . . . " *Friedrich Nietzsche: Philosopher of Culture* (1942: rpt London: Search Press, New York: Barnes & Noble Books, 1975), p. 119.
18. *Twilight of the Idols* in *Twilight of the Idols and The Anti-Christ*, p. 45.
19. *The Anti-Christ* in *Twilight of the Idols and The Anti-Christ*, p. 131.
20. *The Philosophy of Nietzsche*, trans. Horace B. Samuel (1927, rpt. New York: Random House), p. 715.
21. *Collected Papers*, trans. Joan Riviere (1925, rpt. London: Hogarth Press, 1953), IV, p. 215.
22. Ibid., p. 299.
23. *The Major Works of Sigmund Freud*, trans. Joan Riviere, 'Great Books of the Western World', ed. R. M. Hutchins (Chicago: Encyclopedia Britannica, 1952), p. 781.
24. Ibid., p. 788.
25. Ibid., p. 800.
26. *Freud and the 20th Century*, ed. & sel. Benjamin Nelson (New York: Meridian, 1957), p. 20.
27. Letter to Mr. Williams, Charlotte Brontë's publisher. Quoted from *Emily Brontë: A Biography*, Winifred Gerin (Oxford: Oxford University Press, 1978), p. 229.

    Also, according to Elizabeth Gaskell, M. Heger the Belgian professor was greatly impressed by Emily Brontë's intellectual powers. "Emily had a head for logic and a capability of argument unusual in a man and rare indeed in a woman." *The Life of Charlotte Brontë*, ed. Alan Shelston (Harmondsworth Penguin, 1975), p. 230.
28. Wilhelm Nero Pilate Barbellion unwittingly paid a great tribute to Emily Brontë when he made the supposedly disparaging remark in *A Last Diary*. "One might almost write her down as Mrs. Nietzsche . . . no fit companion for the young ladies of a seminary. . . ." Cited in Kate O'Brien's essay "Diaries and Journals" in *The Heritage of British Literature*, Elizabeth Bowen, Anthony Burgess, David Cecil, Graham Greene, Kate O' Brien (London: Thames & Hudson, 1983), p. 215.
29. *The Philosophy of Nietzsche*, trans. Horace B. Samuel (1927; rpt. New York: Random House, 1954), p. 806.
30. All textual references are from the Harmondsworth: Penguin edition of *Wuthering Heights*.
31. *Twilight of the Idols* in *Twilight of the Idols and The Anti-Christ*, p. 45.

32. *Apocalypse* (Harmondsworth: Penguin, 1979), p. 125.
33. *The Letters of D. H. Lawrence,* ed. George J. Zytaruk & James T. Boutton (Cambridge: Cambridge University Press, 1981), II, p. 470.
34. Ibid., p. 470.
35. Ibid., p. 633.
36. Apocalypse, p. 30.
37. Ibid., p. 53.
38. *The Letters of D. H. Lawrence,* ed. James T. Boulton & Lindeth Vasey (Cambridge: Cambridge University Press, 1987), V, p. 262.
39. *Christ and Culture* (London: Faber and Faber, 1952), p. 33
40. *An Essay on Man* (1944, rpt. New Haven: Yale University Press, 1945), p. 4.
41. *Civilisation in Transition,* trans. E.C. Hull (1964; rpt London: Routledge & Kegan Paul, 1974), p. 22. Also, Lymn White describes Christianity as "the most anthropocentric religion the world has ever seen." Cited in *Where The Wasteland Ends,* Theodore Roszak (New York: Doublady & Company, 1972), p. 126.

    Also see George Steiner's *In Bluebeard's Castle—Some Notes Towards the Redefinition of Culture* (London: Faber and Faber, 1974, p. 38 and Camille Paglia's *Sex and Violence, Or Nature And Art* (London: Penguin 60s, 1995), p. 27.

    It is instructive to compare Lawrence's position on this issue with that of Nietzsche and Freud. All of them were greatly concerned with the Christian Commandment 'Love Thy Neighbour' and found it highly unsatisfactory. In Nietzsche's view the Christian love is rooted in self-evasion, and the Christian idealism is nothing but a funking of one's identity. Freud too voices his dissatisfaction with the Christian injunction as it totally disregards the human self. However, while Nietzsche would reject it altogether as the negation of being, Freud sees it as a necessary defence against human aggressiveness. Lawrence's position is closer to Nietzsche's and more consistent than Freud's. Lawrence, like Freud maintains that the Christian love-ideal is a 'lie'; but, unlike Freud, he does not consider it necessary. On the contrary, he believes the violence and destructiveness of the West to be the inevitable consequences of this lie. The World War confirmed Lawrence in this belief.

Chapter 3

PASSION AND CRUELTY IN *WUTHERING HEIGHTS*

IN HIS ESSAY on Emily Brontë in *The Disappearance of God*, J. Hillis Miller writes:

> It was perhaps Aunt Branwell who most directly imposed on the Brontë children notions which might have been held at that time either by a Methodist or by an Anglican influenced by Evangelicalism: the concept of the natural depravity of man, the need for a saving relation to God, the relative unimportance of systematic theology, and the insistence on a few simple ideas such as the view that all pleasure is evil, the notion that all life here must be directed to the ultimate end of salvation, and the idea that only a life of restraint, abnegation and submission to duty will have any chance of reaching that end. . . .[1]

I would like to maintain that Emily Brontë rejects all these values in her novel *Wuthering Heights* though J. Hillis Miller tries to argue the contrary. *Wuthering Heights*, in my opinion, is a total repudiation of the Protestantism imposed on Emily Brontë by Aunt Branwell and/or her father Patrick Brontë. The novel is Emily's counter-argument or, more appropriately, her dream; for whatever her conscious attitude towards her aunt's authoritarian ethic,[2] her unconscious self rejected it and *Wuthering Heights* is the dramatic testimony to such rejection.

What is more, in the puritanic ethic of her aunt and also her father, Emily Brontë encountered the repressive Christian culture of the West, for notions like the natural depravity of man, all pleasure is evil, all life must be directed to the ultimate end of salvation and the glorification of abnegation etc. have shaped the consciousness of the West over the ages. Emily Brontë's personal suffering and deprivation gave her an opportunity to examine an entire culture with a daring and an intensity very few writers are capable of. The nearest parallel in modern times is D. H. Lawrence whose negative experiences with 'spiritual' women led to the rejection of the entire idealistic culture of the west.

J. Hillis Miller in his essay also refers to John Wesley's *On The Education of Children* as a very potent influence on the nineteenth-century England. Wesley's advice to the "wise parent" is that he should begin to break their (children's) will the moment it appears. "Show them that, in pride, passion and revenge they are now like the Devil."[3] Significantly, what distinguishes the children in Emily's novel are their pride, passion and revenge—the Wesley vices.[4] It is hard to think of more unchristian characters than Heathcliff and Catherine. Even Isabella and the young Catherine, who boasts of a "better nature", find revenge sweet.

Wuthering Heights is a dramatization of the nature of passion—its a-moral magnificence and splendour—celebrated in the relationship of Catherine and Heathcliff; it also serves as a focus on the inadequacy of Christian values like duty and humanity, the parental sentiment, and above all the Christian myth of heaven. Vitally, the uncivilized like Heathcliff and Catherine are seen to be superior to the civilized. It is not merely that they are titanic creatures of splendid passion; Emily transcends this romantic perspective. By virtue of their passional authenticity, they are also seen to be more sensitive and vulnerable notwithstanding their solipsism. Also, the civilized ones for all their moderation and humanity do not cease to be cruel. In fact, their repression, their inability "to live their negative instincts",[5] in Jung's phrase, makes them more cruel. Their cruelty is seen to be life-negating serving no therapeutic purpose as it does in the case of 'uncivilized creatures' like Heathcliff and Catherine. Lockwood is the most outstanding example of the first as Heathcliff is of the second, and it is significant that the novel opens with an encounter of these polar opposites.

"Odiously and abominably pagan"—this is how *Quarterly Review*[6] described *Wuthering Heights* in 1848 the year it was published and how right it was! Only, we feel differently about its pagan quality. We find it so daringly, so exhilaratingly pagan. The Christian notions of duty, humanity and life in heaven go bounding like shells exposed to the 'wuthering' heights of Emily Brontë's vision.

* * *

What is it that binds Catherine and Heathcliff? The bond between them is not an intellectual one, theirs is certainly not a 'mental' relationship, Heathcliff has no mind to speak of; and Catherine herself tells him, when he complains of being neglected, that he is no company. "It's no company at all, when people know nothing and say nothing"[7] (p. 110). Again, Catherine is not drawn to him because he is a fine soul or has moral qualities. In fact, she describes him as "a fierce, pitiless, wolfish man" (p. 141) devoid of any moral sense; the only morality he knows is Catherine's displeasure. "I never say to him let this or that enemy alone, because it would be ungenerous or cruel to harm them, I say—'Let them alone', because I should hate them to be wronged. . . ." (p. 141) This is in sharp contrast to the infatu-ated Isabella who nourishes romantic illusions about Heathcliff. What Catherine shares with Heathcliff is a fierce, savage energy[8]— energy which is a-moral and impersonal. Their relationship has nothing to do with accidents of mind and personality. It is significant that the Catherine-Heathcliff relationship is formed in childhood[9] as also the fact that Heathcliff is a gypsy representing a different mode of consciousness.[10] Our first insight into their relationship is provided by Catherine's diary that Lockwood finds accidentally during his forced stay in the little room at Wuthering Heights:

> 'An awful Sunday!' commenced the paragraph beneath. 'I wish my father were back again. Hindley is a detestable substitute—his conduct to Heathcliff is atrocious—H. and I are going to rebel—we took our initiatory step this evening. All day had been flooding with rain; we could not go to church, so Joseph must needs get up a congregation in the garret; and while Hindley and his wife basked downstairs before a comfortable fire—doing anything but reading their Bibles, I'll answer for it—Heathcliff, myself, and the unhappy plough-boy were commanded to take our prayer-books and mount. . . . The service lasted precisely three hours; and yet my brother had the face to exclaim, when he saw us descending—"What, done already?"'
>
> . . . 'I could not bear the employment. I took my dingy volume by the scroop, and hurled it into the dog-kennel, vowing I hated a good book.'
>
> 'Heathcliff kicked his to the same place. Then there was a hubbub!' . . . I reached this book and a pot of ink from the shelf and pushed the house-door ajar to give me light, and I have got the time on with writing for twenty minutes, but my companion is impatient, and proposes that we

> should appropriate the dairy woman's cloak, and have a scamper on the moors, under its shelter. . . . (pp. 62–64).

Their revolt against the tyrannical Hindley and his puritanic crony Joseph is not merely resistance to social injustice, not just an assertion of individual dignity; it is essentially a fight to preserve the kingdom of childhood. Their kicking off "a good book" and their "scamper on the moors"[11] are an affirmation of the passional self.

That Heathcliff represents nature in all its purity—life of the body in Laurentian terms—is established clearly by the crucial meeting between Heathcliff and Catherine when she returns from Thrushcross Grange. Catherine's stay at Thrushcross Grange has transformed the wild girl into a dignified lady anxious that the dogs may not spoil her "splendid garments". The dogs prefigure her meeting with Heathcliff. Even though she embraces him, she finds him dirty. "She gazed concernedly at the dusky fingers she held in her own and also at her dress, which she feared had gained no embellishment from its contact with his" (p. 95). The dogs are almost like Heathcliff's *alter ego.* The link-up between the dogs and Heathcliff is established in the very beginning when Heathcliff tells Lockwood, "Guests are so exceedingly rare in this house that I and my dogs, I am willing to own, hardly know how to receive them" (p. 49). Chapter 7 may then appropriately be called the focal point of the novel; for it brings out the symbolic significance of both Thrushcross Grange and Wuthering Heights. The Grange is obviously the seat of culture from where the wild mate of Heathcliff has picked up good manners, learnt the worth of cleanliness and the beauty of her splendid garments. This world of culture estranges her from Heathcliff and from her own passional self.

I now turn to Catherine's celebrated "I am Heathcliff" speech—the single most important statement about her relationship with Heathcliff:

> I cannot express it, but surely you and everybody have a notion that there is, or should be, an existence of yours beyond you. What were the use of my creation, if I were entirely contained here? My great miseries in this world have been Heathcliff's miseries, and I watched and felt each from the beginning, my great thought in living is himself. If all else perished, and he remained, I should still continue to be; and if all else remained, and he were annihilated, the universe would turn to a mighty stranger:

> I should not seem a part of it. My love for Linton is like the foliage in the woods: Time will change it, I'm well aware, as winter changes the trees. My love for Heathcliff resembles the eternal rocks beneath: a source of little visible delight, but necessary. Nelly, I *am* Heathcliff.[12] (p. 122)

The speech has been interpreted in both Marxist and idealistic terms. The most notable example of the Marxist approach is Arnold Kettle's essay on "*Wuthering Heights*" in *An Introduction to The English Novel*. Kettle remarks:

> He (Heathcliff), the outcast slummy, turns to the lively, spirited, fearless girl who alone offers him human understanding and comradeship. And she born into the world of Wuthering Heights senses that to achieve a full humanity, to be true to himself as a human being, she must associate herself totally with him in his rebellion against the tyranny of the Earnshaws and all that tyranny involves.[13]

What Catherine offers Heathcliff cannot be adequately grasped in terms like "human understanding" and "comradeship". Heathcliff has not much use for human understanding and, as Catherine informs Isabella, is utterly devoid of the moral sense. Infact, Catherine associates with Heathcliff not to "achieve a fully humanity" but because he represents her pre-human nature in all its purity. It is her visit to Thrushcross Grange that "holds Catherine for a human destiny" to borrow that wonderful phrase from Dorothy Van Ghent. The rebellion of Heathcliff and Catherine cannot be grasped in liberal-egalitarian terms; as suggested earlier, it is essentially a fight to preserve the kingdom of childhood. What would their scamper on the moors signify in Kettle's terms? Also, what social or moral significance can be attributed to Heathcliff's association with the dogs?

J. Hillis Miller sees Catherine's speech as "the climax and endpoint of the long tradition making love a private religion in which the loved one is God and there is a single worshipper and devotee".[14] To view the Catherine-Heathcliff relationship thus is to commit a greater fallacy, for that would mean it is the product of a highly sophisticated culture which it decidedly is not. Terms like "private religion" and the "worshipper and devotee" metaphor are loaded with idealistic overtones and can hardly do justice to the fierce, a-moral passion of the Brontë protagonists.

It seems to me that critics like Miller have been misled by Emily's reputation as a mystic. Also, Catherine's jargon—her use of words like "soul" which belong to the idealistic lexicon—tempts one to make that mistake; but here they are merely a part of the common idiom. The speech cannot be isolated from the total context of the novel—its "moorish, and wild and knotty" texture (as Charlotte Brontë noted in her '1850 Preface' to the novel) and the "savage, hardy and free" existence of Catherine that she shares with Heathcliff. Attention must also be paid to the imagery employed by Catherine—the images of foliage and rocks. It is significant that Catherine while talking of Heathcliff does not think of the heavens above as would be in keeping with the conventional mythology of the soul but of the rocks beneath, for what she shares with Heathcliff is not the mind-soul affinity but the passional substructure. Viewed thus, "an existence of yours beyond you" would not refer to a metaphysical essence but to the existence beyond the conscious—the unconscious. This is what she means when she describes Heathcliff as "more myself than I". Heathcliff represents her animal self—her a-moral nature—in all its purity and integrity. This reading of the speech is also backed by Catherine's revelation of her dream a little later:

> . . . heaven did not seem to be my home, and I broke my heart with weeping to come back to earth; and the angels were so angry that they flung me out, into the middle of the heath on the top of Wuthering Heights, where I woke sobbing for joy that will do to explain my secret, as well as the other. I've no more business to marry Edgar Linton than I have to be in heaven. . . . (p. 121)[15]

Heaven cannot be Catherine's home, for heaven is the realm of the disembodies spirit—hence the realm of alienation from the passional self. No wonder Catherine breaks her heart weeping to come back to earth, to Wuthering Heights, to her home.[16] The linking of Edgar Linton with heaven is significant, for both heaven and Linton are instruments of culture and involve repression of the passional self. Edgar Linton is a heaven to which she does not belong. Both heaven and Thrushcross Grange separate her from Wuthering Heights, that is, from her nature. The dignified lady and the disembodied spirit are alike divorced from the bodily self. No wonder Catherine feels later she is married to a stranger and Mrs. Linton appears to her a sort of hallucination:

> . . . I cannot say why I felt so wildly wretched—it must have been temporary derangement for there is scarcely cause—But, supposing at twelve years old, I had been wrenched from the Heights, and every early association, and my all in all, as Heathcliff was at that time, and been converted, at a stroke, into Mrs. Linton, the lady of Thrushcross Grange, and the wife of a stranger; an exile, and outcast, thenceforth from what had been my world. (p. 163)

Here we have what becomes a dominant motif in D. H. Lawrence's fiction—the antagonism between the social and the natural self and the unreality of the former in vitalistic terms. In "St. Mawr", Lou Witt, the female protagonist is awakened to the phantomlike unreality of her social life—"Lady Carrington and all that"—when she encounters the mysterious stallion. In *Lady Chatterley's Lover*, Connie finds Lady Chatterley business a fraud, especially after she comes in contact with the gamekeeper. There is an important difference however. In Lawrence the protagonist is able to discard the unreal social self and preserve the integrity of the natural. In Emily Brontë the claims of the social self cannot be discarded; in fact, their reconciliation is the theme of the latter part of the novel. I shall return to it a little later.

To come back to Catherine's delirium, it (the delirium) not only makes her realize her profound estrangement from her affective self; it also gives her an insight into the seamy side of the Grange. When she imagines Isabella's and Edgar's reaction to her death, she is not indulging in a self-pitying fantasy but comprehending the essential truth of their civilized existence—its complacent rationalization, its use of books, sentiments and otherworldly myths to dodge the agony and passion of man's life. Catherine's apprehension about "Edgar offering prayers of thanks to God for restoring peace to his house, and going back to his books"[17] (p. 160) proves to be right. This is how Edgar is going to 'face' her death—this is how the civilized have always negotiated the death of their beloved ones. Unlike gypsies, they do not put all their eggs in one basket; they have other attachments. The difference between Edgar's civilized affection and Heathcliff's barbaric passion is brought out most effectively by their response to

Catherine's death—a difference which the observant Nelly remarks on while narrating the history of Heathcliff:

> But he was too good to be thoroughly unhappy long. He didn't pray for Catherine's soul to haunt him. Time brought resignation, and a melancholy sweeter than common joy. He recalled her memory with ardent, tender love, and hopeful aspiring to the better world, where, he doubted not, she was gone. (p. 219)

The civilized one like Edgar are "too good" to be unhappy long, for they are amenable to time. Also, to be civilized is to have manifold attachments; in Edgar's case it is love of books and love of his daughter apart from his belief in "the better world". Heathcliff has none of these; hence, his agony which is a measure of his passion. Even though Nelly means it as unqualified praise' her observation has ironical overtones. To be "good" is to be happy, i.e., to renounce one's passion, even sensitivity. The opposite of good here is not bad, but passionate, for Heathcliff's passion is not held out as a wicked thing. Heathcliff's response to Catherine's death vividly conveys the immensity and splendour of his passion. Heathcliff must face the fact of Catherine's death alone and naked. He is more vulnerable than the civilized Edgar, for he has put all his eggs in one basket—his love of Catherine. He has lived solely by his passion for her. He has no human attachments or impersonal interests, as Edgar has to alleviate his suffering. Again, he is not, unlike Edgar, armed with the 'illusion'[18] that Catherine is gone to "the better world". He must feel the full weight of Catherine's death unprotected by any armour-plate of culture, any shockabsorbers provided by civilization. So he must howl in the human jungle like "a savage beast getting goaded to death with knives and spears" (p. 204). The image of the savage beast appropriately conveys both the immensity of Heathcliff's passion and his vulnerability in it. Thus Heathcliff, the uncivilized gypsy, is seen to be more vulnerable than Edgar Linton, the civilized gentleman.

Because of the nature of Heathcliff's suffering one is inclined to agree with him (Heathcliff) when he talks of the superiority of his feeling for Catherine and contemptuously dismisses Edgar's "duty" and "humanity" (Chapter 14). For Heathcliff Edgar's "humanity" and "sense of duty" are poor substitutes for passion—and in all probability this has authorial backing—something one can only "fall back upon". The poverty and bankruptcy of "duty" and "humanity"—the oughts of civilized existence—in vitalistic terms is effectively demonstrated by Catherine's alienation and emotional atrophy. Emily Brontë's affinity with Nietzsche on this point has been noted in the previous chapter.

Not only are civilized morality and the Christian heaven seen to negate the passional self, Emily perceives a basic antagonism between sexual love and love of children. Such is the fierce integrity of her vision, her extraordinary daring, that she boldly confronts the truth about the most sacred of human sentiments, that is, the repressive nature of parental sentiment. For that precisely is the significance of Catherine's taunt to Heathcliff to which he violently reacts:

> . . .Will you say twenty years hence, 'That's the grave of Catherine Earnshaw. I loved her long ago, and was wretched to loser her, but it is past, I've loved many others since—my children are dearer to me than she was, and, at death, I shall not rejoice that I am going to her, I shall be sorry that I must leave them! Will you say so, Heathcliff?' (p. 195)

Catherine's observation reveals the basic antagonism between the nature of sexual passion and the parental bond, between love of woman and the love of children.[19] While the a-social, a-moral sovereignty of the former aligns it with the ecstasy of the mystics and the delight of children; the latter is the surest means of making man a moral creature by subordinating his 'egotistic' impulses to altruistic ends. To love one's child is to subordinate passion to sentiment, to renounce the present and invest in the future. Admittedly, the love of children is a natural instinct, but society places extraordinary value on it and employs it to hold even the most recalcitrant of outlaws for a human destiny.

What the civilized lack in passion and vitality is not necessarily gained by them in humanity. In fact, the civilized ones are seen to be more cruel than the not-so-civilized, for their repressed impulses find devious and destructive expression. Lockwood's cruelty, when he rubs the wrist of the child on the windowpane, springs from his fear of the non-human. The child in the dream is an appropriate symbol of the non-human forces Lockwood—the pun on his name is significant—is trying to keep out. His fear of eros—the most powerful and the most immediate manifestation of the non-human—is earlier seen in his abortive affair with "the most fascinating creature". Again, Isabella, who reminds the reader of the "delicate lady" of Emily's French essay "Le Chat",[20] does not protest when Heathcliff hangs her dog. In fact, he accuses her of having "an innate admiration" of brutality. The callousness implicit in Edgar's response to Catherine's death has already been dealt with.

Wuthering Heights juxtaposes the cruelty of men like Heathcliff against that of the civilized like Lockwood. While Lockwood's cruelty springs from the terror of losing his egotistic identity—"terror made me cruel" (p. 67)—Heathcliff's is a condition of living, that is, of loving Catherine. The younger Catherine provides the right cue when she tells him, ". . . your cruelty arises from your greater misery" (p. 319). In other words, his cruelty is only thwarted eros. Heathcliff's most horrible acts result from the frustration of his hopes of 'meeting' Catherine—for instance, his stamping on the unconscious Hindley. We come to know later in the novel that Heathcliff hoped to meet Catherine's ghost that night at Wuthering Heights and was infuriated by the attempts of Isabella and Hindley to keep him out. That Heathcliff's cruelty is only thwarted eros is finally established when he loses all interest in persecuting the younger Catherine and Hareton towards the end, for he has nearly attained his heaven. His cruelty, then, was only an infernal sport, a means of alleviating his misery. It loses all meaning when the union with Catherine looks imminent.

Heathcliff, however, has wider significance. He is a catalytic agent. What Moby Dick the white whale does to Captain Ahab in Melville's classic, Heathcliff seems to do to those who come in contact with him—to tear off the mask of culture and reduce them to their primal self. It is remarkable that all those who come in contact with him shed their 'culture' a little and become impassioned and aggressive like him: they become imbued with the Heathcliff spirit as it were. Thus Isabella declares her faith in the law of the jungle—"an eye for an eye, a tooth for a tooth" (p. 215). The younger Catherine who claims to have a "better" nature and swears by Christian values derives satisfaction from thinking that Heathcliff's "cruelty arises from your greater misery". And we have Nelly Dean's choral observation, ". . . she seemed to have made up her mind to enter into the spirit of her future family and draw pleasure from the griefs of her enemies." (p. 319). Even Edgar Linton abhors Heathcliff with "an intensity which the mildness of his nature would scarcely seen to allow" (p. 219).

Emily Brontë confronts us with the pagan truth that Christian idealism had persistently, obstinately denied—the truth that under our civilized skins there exists a Heathcliff in us. "Heathcliff is more myself than I am." The greatness of *Wuthering Heights* is owing not a little to this recognition on part of the reader.

However, it would be no one's case that Emily Brontë rejects civilization *per se.* In the drama of the second generation, the author envisages the possibility of an enduring and vital relationship by reconciling passional energy with societal form. When Lockwood suddenly returns to Wuthering Heights and finds the two lovers reading a book, the word that greets his ears is 'contrary':

> 'Con-trary!' said a voice, as sweet as a silver bell—'That for the third time, you dunce! I am not going to tell you, again—Recollect, or I pull your hair!'
>
> 'Contrary, then', answered another, in deep but softened tones. 'And now, kiss me, for minding so well.'
>
> 'No, read it over first correctly, without a single mistake.'
>
> The male speaker began to read: he was a young man, respectably dressed, and seated at a table, having a book before him. His handsome features glowed with pleasure. . . .
>
> The task was done, not free from further blunders, but the pupil claimed a reward, and received at least five kisses: which, however, he generously returned. Then they came to the door, and from their conversation, I judged they were about to issue out and have a walk on the moors. (pp. 338–39)

The choice of the word "contrary" is not without significance, for the younger Catherine and Hareton are trying to reconcile opposites. The books and the moors, which represent antagonistic modes of consciousness in the first part of the novel, are reconciled here. The education of Hareton, and in a sense of the Heights, is conducted by importing not only books but also flowers. Books and flowers have always been considered means and manifestation of culture associated as they are with cultivation of mind and a sense of beauty. It is Catherine's offer of a book to Hareton wrapped in a handsome paper that serves at once as an olive branch and an instrument of civilizing him. Interestingly enough, it is the kicking of a "good book", that had forged the bond between Catherine Earnshaw and Heathcliff earlier.

However, it is not Hareton alone who needs to be educated; Catherine's emotional education is equally important. The most important scene in this connection is in Chapter 23 where we have the total situation of the first generation viewed from a different perspective:

> 'Is the fool drunk?' asked Mr. Heathcliff. 'Hareton, is it you he's finding fault with?'
>
> 'I have pulled up two or three bushes,' replied the young man; 'but I'm going to set'em again.'
>
> 'And why have you pulled them up?' said the master.
>
> Catherine wisely put in her tongue. 'We wanted to plant some flowers there,' she cried. 'I'm the only person to blame, for I wished him to do it.'
>
> 'And who the devil gave you leave to touch a stick about the place?' demanded her father-in-law, much surprised. 'And who ordered you to obey her?' he added, turning to Hareton. . . .
>
> . . . He said he wouldn't suffer a word to be uttered to him in his disparagement: if he were the devil, it didn't signify . . . and then she comprehended that Earnshaw took the master's reputation home to himself; and was attached by ties stronger than reason could break—chains, forged by habit, which it would be cruel to attempt to loosen. (pp. 349–51)

Catherine Linton is as rebellious as her mother. Heathcliff is cast in the mould of the tyrannical Hindley. But Hareton is essentially different from Heathcliff of the first story. Catherine's attempts to rouse him against Heathcliff fail not because Hareton believes in forgiving his enemies but because he is strongly attached to him. Hareton's attachment to Heathcliff seems thoroughly convincing, for the "devil-daddy" is daddy still, and Heathcliff's interest in Hareton saves the latter from complete emotional disintegration and may well be the source of his inherent goodness. Eventually Catherine Linton comes to comprehend the nature of Hareton's attachment and respect it. In Catherine Linton's ability to see that it would be cruel to snap the bond that exists between Hareton and Heathcliff lies a way out of the solipsistic oasis of the elder generation and the possibility of further societal ties.

Catherine's *joie de vivre* is also instrumental in the happy union of the protagonists. Although she nurses her sick husband like a devoted wife, she does not play the martyr to his memory and instinctively turns to Hareton. Interestingly enough, it is frost which thaws the ice between them, and her interest, to begin with, takes the form of adverse criticism. ". . . after a while, she changed her behaviour, and became incapable of letting him alone; looking at him; commenting on his stupidity and idleness; expressing her wonder how he could endure the life he lived—how he could sit a whole evening staring into the fire, and dozing" (p. 341). Also, at a crucial moment in their relationship it is her instinct that helps her comprehend Hareton's real feeling beneath the perverse exterior. "Catherine, by instinct, must have divined it was obdurate perversity, and not dislike, that prompted this dogged conduct; for, after remaining an instant, undecided, she stopped, and impressed on his cheek a gentle kiss" (p. 344).

Although the relationship of Catherine Linton and Hareton Earnshaw does imply the subordination of the passional self to civilizational order—they are to move to Thrushcross Grange after their marriage—it would be perhaps misleading to view, as Richard Chase does, it as "the triumph of the moderate, secular, naturalistic, liberal, sentimental paint of view over the mythical, religious, tragic point of view."[21] The insights of the first part are not invalidated by the second. The relationship between the two parts may be called musical[22] (Emily Brontë was known to be a brilliant musician). The second may be seen as an Apollonian variation on the Dionysian theme of the first throwing into relief the tempestuous nature of the elder protagonists rather than invalidating it.

NOTES AND REFERENCES

1. *The Disappearance of God* (Massachusetts: Harvard University Press), p. 181.
2. However there is evidence to show that even in her personal life Emily Brontë was a rebel. In her book *Emily Brontë: A Chainless Soul* Katherine Frank notes that "Emily was the only Brontë daughter who was exempted from teaching Sunday school and who did not attend church regularly" (London: Hamish Hamilton, 1990), p. 109.

   A little later in the same book, Katherine Frank quotes Ellen Nursey's remark that "Emily was a law unto herself and a heroine in keeping that law", p. 115.
3. Cited from Miller, p. 182.
4. While in Charlotte Brontë's *Jane Eyrc* the little Jane experiences "the strangest sense of freedom, of triumph" when she tastes vengeance in attacking Mrs Reed, its after-flavour, "metallic and corroding, gave me a sensation as if I had been poisoned" (Harmondsworth: Penguin, pp. 39–40). There are no such moral overtones in Emily's portrayal of children.
5. "The dammedup instinct-forces in civilised man are immensely more destructive and hence more dangerous, than the instincts of the primitive, who in a modest degree is constantly living his negative instincts."

   "Apollonian and Dionysian" *Psychological Types*, trans. R.F.E. Hull (1964: rpt. London; Routledge & Kegan Paul, 1974), p. 175.
6. Quoted from Melvin Watson's article, "Wuthering Heights and the Critics", *Nineteenth Century Fiction*, 3 (1949), p. 245.

   Also, Lyn Pykett describes *Wuthering Heights* as an "anti-religious novel" which "presents most conventional religious positions as both imaginatively and morally limited and limiting," *Emily Brontë*, p. 34.
7. All textual references from the Harmondsworth Penguin edition of *Wuthering Heights*.
8. In Augusta the heroine of the Gondal Saga we have Catherine Earnshaw's precursor—a-moral, imperious and impassioned. She deserts Lord Alfred and gives her love to Julius justifying it in elemental terms likening the former to the moon who has been obscured by the sun-like Julius. However, her multitudinous affairs become just two in *Wuthering Heights* and are invested with a deep significance by being related to two aspects of her personality.
9. Both Prof. Jacques Blondel and Georges Bataille consider this of great significance. To quote Georges Bataille, "An Jacques Blondel pointed out (*Emily Brontë, experience spirituelle et creation poetique*), we must always keep in mind that the feelings are formed during Catherine's and Heathcliff's childhood." "Emily Brontë and Evil", *La Litterature et le Mal*, trans. Alastair Hamilton, reprinted in *Emily Brontë: Penguin Critical Anthologies*, p. 154.
10. In its impersonality and elemental vitality, the Catherine-Heathcliff relationship anticipates man-woman relationship in D. H. Lawrence except that the

latter is much less soliptistic. In fact, the Laurentian protagonist can be described as Heathcliff created in adult and not-so-soliptistic terms. His being a gypsy, an outsider to the Christian west, has the same sort of significance as the gypsies in Lawrence's novella, *The Virgin and the Gypsy* and the gamekeeper in *Lady Chatterley's Lover* have.

11. In her love of the moors Catherine Earnshaw is like her creator. Charlotte Brontë once told Elizabetth Gaskell that "my sister Emily loved the moors". *The Life of Charlotte Brontë,* p. 158.
12. Catherine's 'I am Heathcliff' speech seems to have its origin in the poem 'No coward soul is mine' particularly the following lines:

    Though Earth and moon were gone
    And suns and universe ceased to be
    And thou were left alone
    Every Existence would exist in thee.

    However, the poem lacks the power of the Catherine speech which it gathers from the sharply individualized matrix of Catherine-Heathcliff relationship.
13. *An Introduction to the English Novel* (London: Hutchinson University Library 1953), I, pp. 144–45.
14. Miller, p. 175.
15. Catherine's dying speech, ". . . the thing that irks me most is this shattered prison" (p. 196) seams to contradict it. For quite sometime I thought Emily Brontë had imposed her personal beliefs on a dramatic creation. But Heathcliff's reaction to her death 'Why, she's a liar to the end', (p. 204) untied the knot. Heathcliff's belief is also backed by the 'objective' evidence, for Catherine returns to Wuthering Heights as a ghost.
16. Linda Williams' reading of Brontë's poems lends support to my interpretation of *Wuthering Heights.* "She would be a poet of that present moment, evolving earth-bound epiphanies, which celebrate the natural world rather than striving for the transcendental . . . In 'The Old Stoic' (1841) she desires only a 'Chainless soul', not a heavenly transformation—'Leave me the heart that now I bear/And give me liberty.' Freedom is more important than heaven, a sentiment which echoes Catherine Earnshaw's dream in chapter nine of *Wuthering Heights." Victorian Literature from 1830 to 1900,* ed. Jane Thomas (London: Bloomsbury, 1994), p. 51.
17. Q. D. Leavis takes a rather curious view of it: "Catherine feels her husband's intellectual tastes to be rivals—when intolerably provoked by her he returns to his studies; and it is this she thinks of when, on what she feels to be her death-bed, she envisages him with great bitterness as "offering prayers of thanks to God for restoring peace to his house, and going back to his books." (*Lectures in America,* London: Chatto & Windus, 1969, pp. 111–12).

    Catherine is not hostile to learning; only she cannot bear the thought of Edgar absorbed in his books while she is dying. She is revolted by his philosophic detachment which seems heartless to her. Also, the critic posits a rather simplistic relationship between a writer's personal preferences and his/her creation when she observes, "The Emily Brontë who kneaded the dough with a German book propped up before her cannot be supposed to endorse Catherine's hostility to learning." A writer lives by life of the mind. It does not, however, follow that he or she cannot create characters who reject such a life with a certain degree of involvement, even approval. How else would one account for Emily's creation of Heathcliff?

18. The word is used in the same sense as Freud does in *The Future of an Illusion.*
19. Emily Brontë's perception of the a-moral, a-social nature of sexual passion is backed by Freud's observation in *Civilisation and Its Discontents*: ". . . the conflict between civilisation and sexuality is caused by the circumstance that sexual love is a relationship between two people, in which a third can only be superfluous, or disturbing, whereas civilisation is founded in relations between larger group of persons. When a love-relationship is at its height, no room is left for any interest in the surrounding world, the pair of lovers are sufficient unto themselves, do not even need the child they have in common to make them happy." *The Major Works of Sigmund Freud*, 'Great Books of the Western World', ed-in-chief: R. S. Hutchins (Chicago: Encyclopedia Britannica), p. 785.
20. The feeling that Heathcliff's accusation that "no brutality disgusted her (Isabella)" has authorial backing is strengthened by Emily's French essay "Le Chat". Its "delicate lady" has strong affinity with Isabella and could be called her prototype. " 'But', says some delicate lady who has murdered half a dozen lap dogs by sheer affection,' 'the cat is such a cruel beast he is not content to kill his prey, but torments it before its death, you cannot bring this accusation against us.' Pretty near, Madam. Your husband, for example, likes hunting very much but foxes are scarce on his land; he would not be able to enjoy the sport often if he does not manage his resources after this fashion. When he has an animal to its last breath, he pulls it from the mouths of the dogs, and saves it to suffer the same ordeal two or three times more, ending finally in death. *You yourself avoid a bloody spectacle because it wounds your weak nerves . . .*" *Five Essays Written in French*, trans. Lorine White Nagel, with an Introduction and Notes by Fannie E. Ratchford (University of Texas Press, 1948), p. 10.
21. "The Brontës: A Centennial Observance", *The Brontës:* Twentiet Century Views, ed. Ian Gregor (New Jersey: Prentice-Hall, 1970), p. 33.
22. According to Ellen Nussey, "the ability with which she took up music was amazing; the style, the touch, and the expression was that of a professor absorbed heart and soul in his theme." Cited in Robert Wallace's *Emily Brontë and Beethoven* (Athens, Georgia: University of Georgia Press, 1986), p. 153.

Chapter 4

LAWRENCE'S REJECTION OF PLATONIC–CHRISTIAN IDEALISM

WHILE BOTH EMILY Brontë and D. H. Lawrence share the extraordinary ability to transmute personal deprivation into metaphor of cultural malaise, Lawrence has a propensity for intellectual definition we do not find in his predecessor. Owing to this propensity Lawrence sees Western civilization as Jesus-Judas syndrome. Lawrence's novels consistently enact this syndrome. The present discussion, however, confines itself to *The Rainbow,* "St. Mawr", *Lady Chatterley's Lover* and *Women in Love* focussing largely on the last which, I believe, is Lawrence's most central statement on the subject.

Ursula Brangwen—the protagonist of the third generation in *The Rainbow*—throws over French and takes up Botany. (Lawrence himself was a student of Botany and loved flowers.) Ursula's decision to take Botany is an act of profound significance. It implies a rejection of the vulgarity and vanity of anthropocentric consciousness, of living altogether by "the little light of science and knowledge". It also implies an affirmation of the cosmological vision. "This was the one study that lived for her. She had entered into the lives of the plants. She was fascinated by the strange laws of the vegetable world. She had here a glimpse of something working entirely apart from the purpose of the human world" (p. 436).[1]

The study of plants "lives" for her; their laws are strange and "entirely apart from the purpose of the human world". The strange independent world of the plants that neither panders to human needs nor is governed by human laws forces recognition of the non-human on her. It fills her with a sense of wonder and mystery, and it is precisely this wonder and mystery that the anthropocentric consciousness has killed. Its worst manifestation is the reductive mentality of the scientific world-view, for its 'nothing-but' approach is inspired by a desire to conquer nature by desacralizing it. Dr. Frankstone's observation—Frankstone is probably meant to suggest Frankenstein—is a typical example of this approach:

> 'I don't see why we should attribute some special mystery to life. . . . May it not be that life consists in a complexity of physical and chemical activities, of the same order as the activities we already know in science? I do not see really why we should imagine there is a special order of life and life alone.' (p. 440)

Dr. Frankstone's observation reveals the deathly impulse behind "extant consciousness", to borrow a phrase from Lawrence's *Women in Love,* in its denial of "some special mystery of life" and in its desire to reduce life to "a complexity of physical and chemical activities". It is this nekro philosophy—if one may use a neologism—Ursula rejects when she takes up Botany.

Ursula rejects Skrebensky for similar reasons, for Skrebensky in his belief that "fighting is the most serious business there is", in looking forward to his appointment in India is "sidetracking his own soul" and thus denying the mystery of life. ". . . a good deal of social life, and plenty going on—hunting, polo—and always a good horse—and plenty of work, any amount of work" (p. 443).

Lydia Brangwen, Ursula's grandmother, had come to similar conclusions earlier. For Paul Lensky, her first husband, equated life with human effort and thought he was the beginning and the end. "So when he failed in his work, everything failed. He stiffened and died" (p. 258). He committed the Western sin of taking too much upon himself, denying the otherness of his wife and children who were little more than a "part of his baggage". He never knew what his wife Lydia knew that "life must go on", that "the individual effort might fail but not the human joy" (p. 258).

Lensky's deadness to human joy is caused by his anthropocentric consciousness, his living by "the little light of science and knowledge". This results in his alienation from nature and his incapacity to renew himself by any contact with it. It is significant that both Ursula and her grandmother Lydia Brangwen are vivified through their contact with nature: the irrespressible horses which fill Ursula with hope at the end of *The Rainbow* have the same significance as the singing thrushes for her grandmother which compel her to live and marry

Tom Brangwen: "But then one morning there was a light from the yellow jasmine which caught her, and after that, morning and evening, the persistent singing of thrushes from the shrubbery, till her heart, beaten upon, was forced to lift up its voice in rivalry and answer" (p. 54).

In "St. Mawr" the central situation is the fashionable painter Rico's treatment of the horse he buys on the insistence of his wife Lou. The symbol of the stern domineering rider trying to control the recalcitrant horse—which often recurs in Lawrence in some form or the other—seems to fascinate the Western imagination. Freud makes use of it in his essay *The Ego and The Id* to convey the tension that exists between the conscious and the unconscious. In Plato's *Phaedrus* man is likened to a charioteer with two horses. That Lawrence was greatly fascinated by the Phaedrus image and saw in it an effective expression of the Western problem is clear from the discussion that Constance Chatterley has with her husband on the subject in *First Lady Chatterley* (pp. 37–38). Lawrence, in all probability, was influenced by the Phaedrus image when he wrote "St. Mawr". Rico's vicious treatment of St. Mawr is similar to that of the black horse in *Phaedrus:*

> 'Fool!' cried Rico, thoroughly unnerved: he had been terribly sideways in the saddle, Lou had feared he was going to fall. But he got his seat, and pulled the reins viciously, to bring the horse to order, and put him on the track again. St. Mawr began to rear: his favourite trick. Rico got him forward a few yards when up he went again.
>
> 'Fool!' yelled Rico hanging in the air. He pulled the horse over backwards on top of him. (pp. 73–74)

Here is the relevant extract from *Phaedrus:*

> Then the charioteer is worse off than ever; he falls back like a racer at the barrier, and with a still more violent wrench drags the bit out of the teeth of the wild steed and covers his abusive tongue and jaws with blood and forces his legs and haunches to the ground and punishes him sorely.[2]

In Lawrence's employment of the Phaedrus image, if one may say so, the thwarted horse rebels and the rider is over-thrown. For Lawrence knew, on his pulse as it were, that no amount of bullying can tame the black horse, and the history of Western civilization with its love of mankind and its concomitant butchery was a testimony to that. That

Rico's treatment of the horse is meant to have this kind of significance is made quite explicit by Lou's query, "which was wrong, the horse or the rider?" as also by the authorial commentary:

> Mankind no longer its own master. Ridden by this pseudo-handsome ghoul of outward loyalty, inward treachery, in a game of betrayal, betrayal, betrayal. The last of the gods of our era, Judas supreme! (p. 78)

Lawrence sees Western civilization as the Jesus-Judas syndrome. For him, idealism is the villain of the piece—the bullying rider who does not recognize the black horse of passions. Outward loyalty makes inward treachery inevitable, the bullying Jesus calls for the revolt of Judas. "They maintain a lie and so they run amok at last," says Birkin in *Women in Love.*

Earlier, in the "tableau vivant" of a delightful home, and a charming young wife Rico's success as a painter is seen to be fragile and vulnerable, for it is built on a repression of the passional self. Rico is described as "dangerously good", and afraid of himself; for his goodness is a lie that might be blown up by the truth of passional reality. This is a characteristic Laurentian perspective on culture—the fragility of the cultural and intellectual accomplishment when it is based on an exclusion of the passional self. This is seen at its best in Lawrence's portrayal of Hermione and Gerald in *Women in Love.*

It is the fear of the passional self that gives rise to cruelty—"eunuch cruelty" as Lawrence calls it—and it is this cruelty that is expressed in Rico's and Manbys's decision to geld the horse. Lockwood's cruelty in *Wuthering Heights* gives expression to a similar feeling. He feels as much threatened by the waif as Rico and Manbys are by the stallion.

Lou fights to protect the horse for he is a greater mystery than a "clever mind"—"a splendid demon" that startles her out of her wonderless existence and makes her aware of "the triviality and superficiality of her human relationships . . . Rico's wife, young lady Carrington and all that" (p. 22). One thinks of Ursula's encounter with the horses in *The Rainbow* and her grandmother's "answer" to the thrushes.

With *Lady Chatterley's Lover* Lawrence seems to move towards an extremist presentation of his theme. Lawrence here discards the complexity of his earlier works—*The Rainbow* and *Women in Love*—for a greater intensity of effect. The drama centres round a woman who is trapped in a deathly existence and yearns to escape it and finally succeeds in doing so with the help of Mellors the gamekeeper who true to his profession is seen as the preserver of life. *Lady Chatterley's Lover* is closest to Lawrence's story of the same period, *The Man Who Died* and might well be called The Woman Who Escaped Death.

In a novel of this sort there can be no question of sympathy or compassion for someone like Clifford Chatterley, and most criticism of *Lady Chatterley's Lover*, including that of Clifford's paralysis a on this count is misplaced. Critics as different as F. R. Leavis and Eliseo Vivas have found fault with the novel on this score. F. R. Leavis in his essay "The Orthodoxy of Enlightenment" observes:

> As for the treatment of Sir Clifford, the significantly manifest scandal of that can hardly he denied. Professor D. W. Harding, with some irony of understatement, has remarked in the *Spectator* that the burden of symbolic responsibilities laid on Sir Clifford grows unquestionably large.[3]

Similarly, Vivas writes:

> The sketch of Clifford is done without pity or understanding. No mitigation is permitted to soften the defects of the man. The word 'compassion', so fashionable since the last war, is one the critic of Lawrence may forget, for Lawrence's hatred of the Cliffords of the world drained all compassion from his heart.[4]

Words like "pity" and "understanding" are largely irrelevant to our understanding of Clifford Chatterley, and "the burden of symbolic responsibilities laid on Sir Clifford" is not as large as F. R. Leavis and D. W. Harding imagine. Clifford's portrait is meant to convey Lawrence's horror of the Platonic ideal—the ideal of disembodied spirit. Clifford's paralysis is meant to represent precisely this ideal and it is this his cronies—as Connie calls his associates—dream of. Clifford is not meant to win our compassion or understanding, he is there to evoke horror, and horror is not compatible with compassion. Also, the symbolic use of Clifford's paralysis is not as arbitrary or wilful as is often imagined. 'Accidents' in Lawrence's fiction are seldom accidental. In *Women in Love* we have the accident of Gerald killing his brother, and Birkin—a Lawrence spokesman—reflecting if accidents were not part of a coherent whole. Accidents in Lawrence's fiction have the same significance as dreams and slips in Freudian psychology; they are a manifestation of the unconscious. The 'accident' of Clifford's paralysis is the fulfilment of a latent wish. Clifford and his cronies contemplate an ideal world where one could "get rid of one's bodies", "when a women needn't be dragged down by her functions" and "babies could be bred in bottles". "I do think sufficient civilisation ought to eliminate a lot of the physical disabilities" (p. 83), remarks Clifford and he is voicing the aspirations of all his associates—the Wragby elite, Benerleys and Strangeways. He is their leader, their *avant garde*, for he has been able to eliminate his own physical disability with the help of an accident. Clifford's paralysis is thus the culmination of the Platonic ideal—the ideal of disembodied spirit whose classic statement is *Phaedo.* Clifford, like Plato's philosopher, has dishonoured the body. Lawrence, however, sees it not as the crown and glory of his striving, but an unmitigated horror. And it is to his credit that he has been able to convey the horror and monstrosity of the Platonic excursus from the body.

This 'civilized' view of love is rooted in his fear of contact, in his refusal to be in touch. It is this that Connie finds missing in her relationship with Clifford. The same fear of contact finds expression in the witty stories that Clifford writes—"a wonderful display of nothingness"—and also in his love of money that Karl Marx so appropriately called "the alienated ability of mankind". Thus, Clifford's relationship with his wife, the witty stories that he writes and his love of money are all essays in disconnection—abstractions that dodge the passional self.

Lawrence perceives a connection between the bourgeois, industrial obsession with money and the Platonic ideal—both are repressive of the passional self. It is indeed ironical that John Maynard Keynes, the Bloomsbury intellectual and a man as different from Lawrence as one can possibly imagine, comes to a similar conclusion in his essay entitled "Economic Possibilities For Our Grandchildren":

> Perhaps it is not an accident that the race which did utmost to bring the promise of immortality into the heart and essence of our religion has also done most for the principle of compound interest, and particularly loves the most purposive of human institutions.[5]

* * *

Women in Love has too often been read as a denunciation of twentieth century industrial civilization. For F. R. Leavis—the most influential critic on D. H. Lawrence—the novel "contains a presentation of twentieth century England—of modern civilisation".[6] For Graham Hough "the chief subsidiary theme—so powerful at times that it is hardly subsidiary—is a criticism of modern industrial society".[7] In Julian Moynahan opinion the principal statement of the novel is that "a living man or woman who embraces the social destiny offered by industrial Western society in the early twentieth century embraces his own dying".[8] Thus phrases like "twentieth century England", "industrial western civilization" occur with a steady regularity in most critical essays on *Women in Love* ever since Leavis wrote his trend-setting book, *D. H. Lawrence: Novelist.*

This approach, in my opinion, is somewhat simplistic, for it ignores the larger cultural context in which Lawrence places modern industrial civilization. For Lawrence, industrial civilization is not a received fact and, contrary to what Raymond Williams says in his book *Culture and Society,*[9] he is interested in its origins. For Lawrence, the industrial civilization is the culmination of the Western anthropocentric consciousness—the Christian-Platonic adventure; and it is this that he rejects in his work, and most significantly in *Women in Love.* Gerald's religion of the machine, for example, can only be understood in the context of Thomas Crich's doctrine of charity. Hermione's intellectuality and ideal love that she offers Birkin are manifestations of a deeper malady than the critique of industrialism implies. Also, Gudrun's tragedy—the tragedy of acute consciousness estranging one from living—is not necessarily a product of the industrial West.

I take *Women in Love* to be the most devastating indictment of Western consciousness—the entire Christian–Platonic adventure by the light of which the Western man has lived for some three thousand years. The chief embodiments of this consciousness are Gerald, Hermione and Gudrun—people who are trying to live by will or/and mind excluding the non-rational, the unconscious. Notwithstanding important differences they are all prisoners of the anthropocentric consciousness. Ursula and Birkin are seen to be the torch-bearers of a new conciousness. What distinguishes them from the civilized ones like Gerald, Gudrun and Hermione is their naivety, their earnestness and their refusal to funk the animal. This leads to Birkin's breaking with Hermione, to Ursula and Birkin giving up their jobs and committing themselves to a final relationship. However, they shall be discussed in the next chapter. The present discussion restricts itself to the consequences of the dominance of anthropocentric consciousness both in man-woman relationship and in the realm of purposive social activity. While the former can best be understood with reference to Birkin-Hermione and Gerald-Gudrun relationships, the latter would require an analysis of Gerald's religion of the machine, Gudrun's cult of art and Hermione's commitment to knowledge.

In an essay entitled "The Revolt of the Body" Octavio Paz writes, "The relationship between non-body and body in European erotic works takes the form: torture/orgasm. Death spurs pleasure and rules over life. From De Sade to the 'Story of O' eroticism is a funeral chant or a sinister pantomime. The body becomes knife or stone. . . ."[10]

In Birkin-Hermione and Gerald-Gudrun relationships Lawrence is portraying two forms of deadly 'white' love—the spiritual love which denies the body, and the sensuous—-a pejorative term with Lawrence—which dehumanizes it. Both however are products of the conscious self and lack spontaneity involving as they do a repression of the unconscious. The knife image that Paz uses in his essay applies perfectly to the Gerald-Gudrun relationship and Lawrence himself uses similar images. The higher love of Birkin and Hermione is stone-like not only in its feelingless denial of the body but also in its bulldozing spirituality which denies 'otherness'.

Birkin's diagnosis of Hermione's spiritual love—a diagnosis which applies equally to Birkin's case with the difference that he is trying to fight if off—is given to us in the chapter 'Class-Room'. Hermione's "passion" is seen to be a "bullying will"—and it is this that Birkin is fighting:

> 'But you passion is a lie', he went on violently. 'It isn't passion at all; it is you will. It's you bullying will. You want to clutch things and have them in your power. You want to have things in your power. And why? Because you haven't got any real body, any dark sensual body of life. . . .' (p. 46).

Hermione offers Birkin, as Graham Hough remarks, "a love which is cut off from the natural carnal roots of love, and continues to exist simply as a function of the will."[11] In the chapter 'Class-Room' we see Birkin revolting against this which partly accounts for the fury of Birkin's attack. Hermione's spirituality is nothing but bullying will, and it is rooted in her lack of sensuality—always a term of appreciation with Lawrence—in her incapacity to be physical. Lawrence dealt with what may be called the Hermione malady earlier in the portrayal of Miriam in *Sons and Lovers.* Indeed in her rhapsodic manner, her drugged gait, her ecstatic absorption in flowers and, finally, in her self-righteous faith in her higher knowledge, Hermione is strongly reminiscent of Miriam. She may be described as a more aggressive Miriam with cultural pretensions. Her domineering nature is suggested by little incidents like her ecstatic attention to flowers ('little red flames', 'little red flames') and by her talking to the deer as if he were a boy, which reminds one of Miriam hugging her little brother in *Sons and Lovers.*

The bullying nature of her love is revealed in her desire to know everything that Birkin does. Her obsession, with every little detail of Birkin's inner life is seen as insane, a psychic compulsion born of an emotional void. Her insane will rooted in a deep emotional void is effectively conveyed by her ecstatic exclamations ('Yes! how beautifully you do it!'), by her interrogations ('You like it very much, don't you?'), by her suggestions and so on:

> 'Your are copying the drawing,' she said, standing near the table, and looking down at his work, 'Yes, how beautifully you do! You like it very much, don't you?'
>
> 'It is a marvellous drawing,' he said.
>
> 'Is it? I am glad you like it, because I have always been fond of it. The Chinese ambassador gave it me.'
>
> 'I know,' he said.
>
> 'But why do you copy it?' She asked, casual and sing-song. 'Why not do something original?'
>
> 'I want to know it', he replied, 'one gets more of China, copying this picture, than reading all the books.'
>
> 'And what do you get?' (pp. 98–99)

Hermione sees Birkin's belief in 'otherness' declared later during the course of a discussion and manifest specifically in his copying the Chinese drawing as a threat to her anthropocentric consciousness. "I know what centres they life from . . . the hot stinging centrality of a goose in the flux of cold water and mud" (p. 97). The Chinese drawing is not accessible to Hermione's mode of knowing. In a sense, Hermione's attempt to knock down Birkin with a paperweight is a desperate act of self-defence. ". . . she must break him down before her, the awful obstruction of him who obstructed her life to the utmost. It must be done, or she must perish most horribly" (p. 117).

Thus the ideal love that Hermione offers Birkin is seen as a manifestation of "extant consciousness" in the personal realm. "To me the pleasure of knowing is so great, so wonderful nothing has meant so much to me in all life, as certain knowledge—no—I'm sure—nothing" (p. 95). The truth about this pleasure of knowing is revealed immediately. When she invites her guests to see the daffodils—an invitation Birkin refuses and others accept as prisoners—Hermione in seen as a jailer who imprisons others with her domineering presence and her prying consciousness.

Gudrun's acute self-consciousness and Gerald's bullying will turn their relationship into a deadly nerve-tearing combat. To be sure, Birkin-Ursula relationship is not free from conflict; their quarrels in fact are far more savage than those of Gerald and Gudrun. The quarrels between Gerald and Gudrun are more in the nature of a cold war fought with all the cunning and diplomatic skill at their command; they are an eternal see-saw which leaves the antagonists emotionally exhausted and satisfies only one's ego or mental consciousness.

For Gudrun, Gerald is "the exquisite adventure". The postlapsarian nature of her experience is vividly rendered in 'Death And Love'.

> She reached up, like Eve reaching to the apples on the tree of knowledge, and she kissed him, though her passion was a transcendent fear of the thing he was, touching his face with her infinitely delicate, encroaching wondering fingers. Her fingers went over the mould of his face, over his features. How perfect and foreign he was—ah, how dangerous! Her soul thrilled with completed knowledge. This was the glistening forbidden apple, this face of a man. (p. 374)

This is a crucial passage. It defines the highly conscious, mental nature of the exquisite adventure that Gerald constitutes for Gudrun. Her artistic detachment and inquisitiveness are conveyed by the reference to her "delicate, encroaching, wondering fingers". She is at once linked up with Eve, and Gerald is the forbidden apple; the image of the forbidden apple conveys a suggestion of damnation. Right in the first chapter, we have Gudrun watching the wedding guests with the "objective curiosity" of an artist. We also come to know she is an artist—a sculptor of some repute. "She saw each one as a complete figure, life a character in a book, or a subject in a picture, or a marionette in a theatre, a finished creation. She loved to recognize their various characteristics, to place them in their true light, give them their own surroundings, settle them for ever as they passed before her along the path to the church. She knew them, they were finished, sealed, and stamped" (p. 15).

It is significant that Gudrun sees each one as a complete figure—the perspective of an artist. She uses her artistic perspective to place them and finish them, to emotionally dispose them off and thus to preserve her own autonomy. Her detachment and objective curiosity are rooted in her self-consciousness; and to this we must turn.

Birkin's response to Gerald's query in the chapter called 'Breadalby' as to whether Gudrun will make a great artist provides a useful clue to Gudrun's mental makeup. Birkin does not believe that she will make a great artist because "She won't give herself away—She's always on the defensive" (p. 105). 'Waterparty' brings out Gudrun's self-consciousness remarkably well where we see the two sisters having a little picnic by themselves. Ursula's spontaneity and joyous absorption in the moment throws Gudrun's acute self-consciousness into sharp relief—a self-consciousness which makes her envious of her sister, incapable as she is of living in the present. Ursula is a perfect foil to Gudrun. "Ursula seemed so peaceful and sufficient unto herself, sitting there unconsciously crooning her song, strong and unquestioned at the centre of her own universe. And Gudrun felt herself outside. Always this desolating, agonised feeling, that she was outside of life, an onlooker, whilst Ursula was a partner, caused Gudrun to suffer from a sense of her own negation, and made her, that she must always demand the other to be aware of her, to be in connection with her" (p. 185).

While Ursula can give herself to the song she is crooning, Gudrun makes deliberate effort to be in touch with her. Ever her wish to dance is thwarted by her self-consciousness. Ursula's "childish surprised brightness" forms a striking contrast to Gudrun's "tortures of self-consciousness".

> 'Do you mind if I do Dalcroze to that tune, Hurtler?' she asked in a curious muted tone, scarce moving her lips.
>
> 'What did you say?' asked Ursula, looking up in peaceful surprise.
>
> 'Will you sing while I do Dalcroze?' said Gudrun, suffering at having to repeat herself.
>
> 'Ursula thought a moment, gathering her straying wits together.
>
> 'While you do—?' She asked vaguely.
>
> 'Dalcroze movements,' said Gudrun, suffering tortures of self-consciousness, even because of her sister.
>
> 'Oh, Dalcroze I couldn't catch the name. Do—I should love to see you,' cried Ursula, with childish surprised brightness. (p. 185)

Gudrun's desire to get over her self-consciousness finds expression in 'Coal-Dust' when she momentarily comes under Gerald's spell who is taming his Arab mare. She experiences tremendous satisfaction by identifying herself with the mare and submitting imaginatively to Gerald's control. This is the only way a highly carebral, repressed, Gudrun can overcome her alienation—by numbing her consciousness. "Gudrun was as if numbed in her mind by the sense of indomitable soft weight of the man, bearing down into the living body of the horse . . ." (p. 126). This links her with Minette the model Gerald meets in London. But Gudrun is more complex than Minette. She has at the same time a desire to conquer Gerald. This is the significance of her dance before Gerald's bullocks. That the bullocks represent for her Gerald and his masculinity is clear from the sexual connotations of the description and Gudrun's retort. "You think I'm afraid of you and you cattle." Gudrun's dance is an invitation and a challenge to the bullocks and hence to their master to engage in a sexual combat. It is also an asertion of her female power—her desire to play the top-dog. That, I believe, is the significance of Gudrun "lifting her body towards them as if in a spell". Together 'Coal-Dust' and 'Water-Party' define the sadomasochistic pattern of her response to Gerald.

For Gerald loving is a form of killing. Gerald's necrophilia finds its manifestation in his affair with Minette the London model introduced by Birkin. He sees her as a victim, and Minette's slavelike nature stimulates the murderous passion of Gerald. "He felt an awful, enjoyable power over her, an instinctive cherishing very near to cruelty. For she was a victim. He felt that she was in his power, and he was generous. The electricity was turgid and voluptuously rich, in his loins. He would be able to destroy her utterly in the strength of his discharge" (p. 71).

The same destructive impulse manifests itself in his relation with Gudrun, but Gudrun is no Minette; hence the drama of their emotional engagement is more intricate.

The complete lack of duality in their relationship is presented most effectively in 'Death and Love'. Gerald goes to Gudrun not for love but for vindication, an emotional release that leaves her entirely out of count. He is seen alternately as the bully and the infant, in either case oblivious of the other party. "He had come for vindication. She let him hold her in his arms, clasp her close against him. He found in her an infinite relief. Into her he poured all his pentup darkness and corrosive death. . . ." (p. 388)

The necrophilic nature of Gerald's passion comes into the open in his adventure with Gudrun in the Alps when he finds she is no Minette. He must reduce Gudrun to a Minette and prove his godhead in her death if not in her life, so he resolves to kill her. For to kill her is to have her, to impose his will on her finally just as he did it earlier with the miners with the help of the machine. His love of death which robbed the mines of all joy and life manifests itself in Gerald's desire "to strangle every spark of life out of her, till she lay completely inert, soft relaxed for ever, a soft heap lying dead between his hands, utterly dead" (p. 518).

Significantly, Gerald's attempt to strangle her and her struggling are described in terms of sexual intercourse. "And her throat was beautiful, so beautifully soft, save that, within, he could feel the slippery chords of her life. . . . The struggling was her reciprocal lustful passion in this embrace, the more violent it became the greater the frenzy of delight. . . ." (p. 531)

This is the nearest they come to an orgiastic release. Their subconscious desire for pseudo-dionysian orgies is thwarted by their own nature—by Gerald's bullying will and Gudrun's self-consciousness. "All that and more" says Gudrun perceiving a kinship with the rabbit who first resists their (Gudrun's and Gerald's) attempt to be drawn out and then bursts into frenzied motion. The rabbit becomes an effective symbol of Gerald's and Gudrun's craving for a mindless experience; it also becomes a sort of objective correlative for the civilized man's dilemma, of one who alternates between tame conformity and savage outbursts. In an extremely perceptive essay on *Women in Love*, Richard Drain observes:

> The contained or imprisoned energies gather in the static animal; dragged out to be drawn, as the dog Loloo has just been drawn—to be, that is, once more contained, delineated, reduced—the energies explode in a destructive yet entirely futile outburst. But once they are expended, the rabbit settles back into harmless domestication.[12]

Drain sees in the rabbit's outburst "a sardonic yet frightening commentary on twentieth century man". The rabbit becomes a totem of the twentieth century civilization with its diabolic efficiency and order on the one hand and its pseudo-Dionysian orgies of lust and violence on the other. Any civilization that represses the passional self makes the orgiastic release inevitable. Orgies are a necessary consequence of the civilizing process. It is significant that Gudrun's craving for a "brutal and licentious" release is stimulated by her thinking of "the abandonments of Roman licence" (p. 324). The recalling of the Roman orgies underlines once again the highly mental nature of Gudrun's "black passion"; it has a respectable historical precedent. Also, the reference to one of the most advanced civilizations helps to establish the universal validity of Lawrence's diagnosis; the imperial ethic of the Roman Empire was as repressive as the Protestant ethic of modern industrial civilization.

I now turn to Gerald's social life—to Gerald, the captain of industry. This must start with his father, Thomas Crich, as Lawrence is concerned with the origins of Gerald's religion of the machine.

Gerald's father Thomas Crich is a Christ-figure. He lives by "charity" and love of the neighbour. "He had been so constant to his lights, so constant to charity and to his love for his neighbour" (p. 241). His wife Christiana finds his philanthropy humiliating and opposes him like one of the demons of hell. She sees that it is parasitic encouraging "the worst sort" of people, "the whining, parasitic, foul human beings" (p. 242), while the proud ones stay away. In his charity, his desire to alleviate the sufferings of the poor, Christiana finds a necrophilic drive—a love of death. Her husband appears to her "some subtle funeral bird, feeding on the miseries of the people". "He would have no *raison d'etre* if there were no lugubrious miseries in the world, as an undertake would have no meaning if there were no funerals" (p. 244). The images of the "funeral bird" and the "undertaker" convey the basic impulse behind Crich's Christianity, namely, its necrophilia.

Christiana is her husband's first victim. "She had beat against the bars of his philanthropy, and like a hawk in a cage she had sunk into silence. By force of circumstances, because all the world combined to make the cage unbreakable, he had been too strong for her, he had kept her prisoner" (p. 242). She recoils away from her husband's creeping democracy but can do nothing as he is ruled by the lie of Christian charity. The self-deception and horror of his idealism is best revealed in his maintaining "how happy he had been, how he had loved her with a pure and consuming love ever since he had known her" (p. 345) and in his belief that "her subjugation"—a subjugation which has driven her insane—was an "infinite chastity".

Gerald's religion of the machine brings out into the open his father's latent necrophilia. It seems to me that neither Daleski nor Leavis show adequate appreciation of the central connection between Thomas Crich's doctrine of charity and Gerald's religion of the machine. Daleski describes Crich's charity as just "corrupting in its effects" and stimulating "a mutual parasitism between donor and recepient"[13] and for Leavis Gerald's taking over the mines simply means that "Thomas Crich's idealism" has resulted in "the triumph of mechanism".[14] It may be useful to recall Lawrence's essay "Making Love To Music" in this connection:

> We become what we think. Worse still, we have become what our grandmothers thought. And our children's children will become lamentable things that we are thinking. Which is the psychological visiting of the sins of the fathers upon the children. For we do not become just the lofty or beautiful thoughts of our grandmothers. Alas no! We are the embodiments of the most potent ideals of our progenitors.[15]

This is of a special relevance to Gerald. He owns "the most potent ideal" of his progenitor—his love of death; for his religion of the machine is nothing but a cleaner death-worship—the same as motivated his affair with Gudrun, and with Minette earlier. We are told very early in the novel that he killed his brother accidentally when he was a boy. In the same chapter 'Shortlands', Birkin, whose observations have choral significance, tells Gerald in so many words, "You have a lurking desire to have your gizzard slit, and imagine every man has his knife up his sleeve for you" (p. 37). Gerald's mother, Christiana, remarks that "he is the most wanting of them all" and that he has never had a friend. She is most anxious about Gerald's well-being when her husband is dying. "Let the dead bury their dead—don't go and bury yourself along with them—that is what I tell you. I know you well enough" (p. 319).

It is this necrophilia which motivates his adventure in the mines. "He had all his life been tortured by a furious and destructive demon which possessed him sometimes like an insanity. This temper now entered like a virus into the firm, and there were cruel erruptions. . . ." (p. 257). Gerald becomes the high priest of a new religion which conceives of human history as the history of conquest of matter by man and celebrates the supreme triumph of the will of man. The miners submit to Gerald because they see it as such. "He merely represented the miners in a higher sense when he perceived that the only way to fulfil perfectly the will of man was to establish the perfect inhuman machine" (p. 257).

To impose one's will over man and matter is to achieve godhead, to demonstrate that man is the lord of creation, and thus to fulfil the Biblical prophecy. Thus the machine is the culmination of anthropocentric consciousness. The machine is like a parallel creation—man becoming his own god, and severing himself from the unknown. Gerald is the diabolic priest and he succeeds since the miners derive a satanic satisfaction out of the whole enterprise. "The men were satisfied to belong to the great and wonderful machine, even whilst it destroyed them. It was what they wanted. It was the highest that man had produced, the most wonderful and super-human. They were exalted by belonging to the great and superhuman system which was beyond feeling or reason, something really godlike. Their hearts died within them, but their souls were satisfied" (p. 260).

I shall now briefly discuss Gudrun's cult of art and Hermione's love of knowledge to examine the application of the Western world-view to the realm of art and ideas. "Isn't it queer that she always likes little things?—She must always work small things, that one can put between one's hands, birds and tiny animals" (p. 42), says Ursula of her sister's art. Presumably, Gudrun likes to make little things—things that one can put between one's hands—so that she can feel like a goddess. By creating little things she becomes their goddess; she gets a feeling of mastery and domination shutting off all sense of awe and mystery.

Gudrun's interest in carving little things is inspired by the same impulse as makes her seek an alliance with Loerke—who is truly her comrade-in-arms, her *glucksritter*—and play art-games. "They played with the past and with the great figures of the past, a sort of little game of chess, of marionettes, all to please themselves. They had all the great men for their marionettes, and they two were the God of the show, working it all" (p. 509).

In Gudrun and Loerke we have the artist-god just as Gerald is the god of the industrial show. Like Gerald, they commit the anthropocentric sin enacting the Laurentian paradox that men who try to be gods lose their creativity—their sense of wonder and mystery. Their alliance is a mutual vindication of each other's cynical rejection of living. This is what impels Loerke to make his life-negating distinction between "the relative work of action" and "the absolute world of art" which, as Ursula is quick to perceive, is a flight from the self; Loerke has to separate the two "because you can't bear to know what you are" (p. 485).

Gudrun needs an intellectual justification for her way of living (or non-living). And that is what she finds in Loerke. She feels a tremendous sense of elation and freedom when Loerke dismisses life as a bagatelle:

> 'Or course,' said Gudrun, 'life does not really matter—it is one's art which is central. What one does in one's life has *peu de rapport*, it doesn't signify much.'
>
> 'Yes, that is so, exactly,' replied the sculptor. 'What one does in one's art, that is the breath of one's being. What one does in one's life, that is a bagatelle for the outsiders to fuss about.' (p. 504)

Lawrence's aversion to Flaubertian art is well-known, and in portraying Gudrun and Loerke he must have had in mind the Flaubertian approach to art and its twentieth century exponents in England—the Bloomsbury intellectuals. Ursula's retort ends with the characteristic Laurentian observation. "The world of art is only the truth about the real world . . ." (p. 485).

Right in the first chapter, 'Sisters', we are told that Hermione was a "*Culturtrager*, a medium for the culture of ideas. With all that was highest whether in society or in thought or in public action, or ever in art, she was at one with; she moved among the foremost, at home with them" (p. 17). But all her cultural defences collapse when Birkin tries to break away from her, and we see the predatory female, behind the cultural facade, who must clutch things and people and smash them when thwarted. Commenting on her knocking down Birkin with a paper-weight Graham Hough aptly remarks, "Hermione who attempts to live entirely in the mind and the spirit, to frame a world of aesthetic and universal emotions is betrayed into an act of vulgar physical violence."[16]

Similarly, her interest in Barnes' aesthetics and Olandese's politics does not prevent her from envying Ursula's "unconscious positivity" even her "vulgarity". The two—her envy of Ursula's "vulgarity" and her cultural interests—are very effectively juxtaposed in 'Woman to Woman', where Hermione makes her last appearance.

This is the characteristic Laurentian perspective on culture. Civilized existence is seen to be fragile and even barren when it is divorced from the passional self. So when Birkin denounces Hermione for her advocacy of spontaneity and animalism, he is justified. Hermione's animalism, as Birkin puts it is "the worst and last form of intellectualism." "It's all that Lady of Shalott business. You have got that mirror, your own fixed will, your immortal understanding, your own tight conscious world, and there is nothing beyond it" (p. 45). The Lady of Shalott metaphor pins down the extraordinary narcissism and highly mental gratification to be derived from this going-back-to-nature—this self-conscious primitivism. This is the civilized disease at its worst. What an irony Lawrence himself should have been accused of it! The cult of the primitive, however, is a product of the repression of the animal—of over-civilization. The civilized ones like Gudrun, Hermione and Gerald are seen to be particularly vulnerable to the lure of the pseudo-Dionysian orgy; the thwarted animal must assert itself with a vengeance. So, although, *Women in Love* is not a novel about "repudiation of mind in an extreme of abandonment to frenzied sexuality and the Dark Gods",[17] as Leavis points out, it certainly makes a case for a different relationship with the Dark Gods. And this relationship shall be the subject of our next chapter.

NOTES AND REFERENCES

1. All textual references are from the Harmondsworth Penguin editions of Lawrence's works except in the case of *Lady Chatterley's Lover* where the Cardinal edition, New York (July, 1959) has been used.
2. *Dialogues of Plato*, trans. Benjamin Jowett (Chicago: Encyclopedia Britannica, 1952), p. 224.
3. *Anna Karenina And Other Essays* (London: Chatto & Windus, 1967), p. 240.
4. *D. H. Lawrence: The Failure and The Triumph of Art* (London: George Allen & Unwin, 1961), p. 122.
5. *Essays in Persuasion, The Collected Writings of John Maynard Keynes* (1931; rpt London & Basingstoke: MacMillan; 1972), IX, p. 330.
6. *D. H. Lawrence: Novelist* (1955; rpt Harmondsworth: Penguin, 1969), p. 178.
7. *The Dark Sun* (London: Gerald Duckworth), p. 73.
8. *The Deed of Life* (Princeton: Princeton University Press, 1963), p. 88.
9. "Lawrence is little concerned, historically, with the origins of industrialisation. For him, in this century it is a received fact. . . ." *Culture and Society 1780-1950* (London: Chatto & Windus, 1958), p. 202.
10. Hudson Review, 23 (1970-71), p. 656.
11. *The Dark Sun*, p. 243.

12. *D. H. Lawrence*, ed. A. H. Gomme (1978; rpt Sussex: Harvester Press, 1979), p. 84.
13. *The Forked Flame: A Study of D. H. Lawrence* (London: Faber & Faber, 1965), p. 144.
14. *D. H. Lawrence: Novelist*, p. 195.
15. *Phoenix: The Posthumous Papers of D. H. Lawrence*, ed. Edward McDonald (Harmondsworth: Penguin, 1978), p. 160.
16. *The Dark Sun*, p. 87.
17. *D. H. Lawrence: Novelist*, p. 179.

Chapter 5

LAURENTIAN ALTERNATIVE: THE NON-HUMANIST VISION

THE CARDINAL SIN of the Western consciousness is, as I argued in the last chapter, that it robbed men of all wonder and mystery—the Laurentian *sine qua non* of life—one, by repressing and bullying the passional self and two, by making man the measure of all things. Does Lawrence offer a way out of the Western *cul de sac*?

There can be little doubt that Lawrence is not just "a maker of wasteland novels".[1] The Platonic-Christian adventure of three thousand years stood indicted because it left out the non-human, and made man's existence all too human. Lawrence's entire life and work was a quest for a way out of the Western *cul de sac.* His "savage pilgrimage", his fascination for Mexico and Etruscan places, his love of gypsies and gamekeepers, his forays into anthropology were all inspired by his desire to find clues to a new way of life—to find a way out of the claustrophobia and ennui of the Western consciousness. As early as 1914, Lawrence said in a letter to Gordon Campbell:

> Then the vision we're after, I don't know what it is—but it is something that contains awe and dread and submission, not pride or sensuous egotism and assertion. I went to the British Museum—and I know, from the Egyptian and Assyrian sculpture—what we are after. We want to realise the tremendous non-human quality of life—it is wonderful. It is not the emotions, nor the personal feelings and attachments that matter. These are all only expressive, and expression has become mechanical: Behind it all are the tremendous unknown forces of life, coming unseen and unperceived as out of the desert to the Egyptians, and driving us, forcing us, destroying us if we do not submit to be swept away.[2]

It is realization of "the tremendous non-human quality of life"—the realization that we are not the great choosers we think we are, that the body has a life of its own and that "man does not live by man alone"[3]—that impels Lawrence to reject Western civilization. Also, this necessitated a different relationship both with the passional self and the non-human universe. I shall be studying Lawrence's view of man's relation with the passional self with reference to Birkin-Ursula relationship in *Women in Love* and Connie-Mellors relationship in *Lady Chatterley's Lover.* The second—man's relation with the non-human universe—though spread all over Lawrence's œurve can be studied with advantage in the short story "Sun" and the novella "St. Mawr" as both of them have non-human protagonists.

In *The First Lady Chatterley* there is a conversation between Clifford Chatterley and his wife which could serve as a useful starting point for our discussion. The conversation centres on Plato's treatment of the black horse in *Phaedrus*:

> 'Don't you think it's rather cruel, the way Socrates drives his black horse—jerking him till his mouth and tongue are full of blood, and bruising his haunches? Don't you think one could manage a horse better than that?
>
> Clifford looked at her keenly. She had found the taint of bullying, even in Socrates. Even Socrates was a bully! And in her heart of hearts Constance was quite determined against any sort of bullying.
>
> 'Perhaps not a vicious horse,' he said.
>
> 'But perhaps Blackie isn't so vicious. Don't you think, if one asked him what he truly wanted , he's as much right to it as the white horse or the driver? Only Socrates thinks he must have his mouth cut and be thwarted.' . . .
>
> 'You would say the black horse has a right to all his desires?' he asked.
>
> 'Well, wouldn't you? Only at the right time in the right order. Don't you think, instead of the white horse and the driver both struggling to thwart the black one, they should say to him: Gently! Gently! Go gently, and we'll go with you! Go quietly, without overturning the chariot, and we'll drive right into the place you want.'
>
> He looked at her shrewdly.
>
> 'Do you think it would answer?' he said.
>
> 'Why shouldn't it,' she said. 'Either the black horse has a perfect right to his own existence and his own desires and gratifications, or he shouldn't exist. . . .'[4] (pp. 37–38)

One could legitimately assume that Constance here represents the author, for here we have the key Laurentian ideas thrown together, namely, that Plato-Socrates is unjust to the black horse, that the black horse is not vicious and must be treated differently, and finally the characteristic Laurentian argument in defence of the black horse. "Either the black horse has a perfect right to his own existence or he shouldn't exist." In Constance's view, and in D. H. Lawrence's perhaps, the very existence of the black horse constitutes an argument against its denial. The black horse *is there*—it isn't there for thwarting. The body has a life of its own and must be allowed to live that life. In other words, to thwart the black horse is to go against nature; to deny the isness of things is to invite disaster.

Lawrence's work must be viewed as an attempt to make friends with the black horse. To make friends with the black horse is to accept the sensuality of love, to accept without shame and guilt the bestial and even the so-called perverse, and above all to accept that conflict and even hatred form a part of man-woman relationship. Barbara Hardy draws our attention to this aspect of Lawrence's achievement in her book, *The Appropriate Form:*

> One of his most important contributions to the realism of fiction, in theory and in practice, is his rejection of the kind of specialised emotion which is the basis of the Victorian novel and of many twentieth century delineations of love. . . . In *Women in Love* Lawrence shows a multiplicity of emotion in the central relation between Birkin and Ursula. There is tenderness, loving intimacy, the impersonal 'bestial' passion and a constant struggle.[5]

Every Laurentian protagonist makes the great discovery that there is "something else beside the personality" and the body has a "life of its own"[6] (*The First Lady Chatterley*, p. 29). This is the discovery Paul makes in *Sons and Lovers* when he goes to Clara for his baptism of passion; this is *also* the discovery the protagonist of *The Man Who Died* makes when he wakes to the wonder of the phenomenal world and encounters the Lady of Isis. Again, the discovery of one's body is made not with a sense of shame or guilt but with awe and wonder. The protagonist feels reborn or metamorphosed as it were. For Connie Chatterley the sight of the gamekeeper washing himself is a "visionary experience". This visionary experience hits her in the middle of her body and makes her aware of her own impoverished existence. When she goes home she takes off her clothes, and looks at herself naked in the mirror. "Her body was going meaningless, going dull and opaque, so much insignificant substance. It made her feel immensely depressed and hopeless. What hope was there? She was old, old at twenty—even, with no gleam and sparkle in the flesh. Old through neglect and denial, yes denial" (p. 79).

Now she decides to fight Clifford and his consciousness, for the life of the body has been thwarted by the deadwood of ideas and ideals. And Constance has the instinct to see Clifford as the enemy—one who would turn her life into an abstraction just as he turns violets into "Juno's eyelids." "Suddenly, with all the force of her female instinct, she was shoving him off. She wanted to be clear of him, and especially of his consciousness, his words, his obsessing with himself, his endless treadmill obsession with himself, and his own words" (p. 105).

Thus, we see Connie Chatterley moving away from the world of Clifford who, like Phaedo's philosopher, "disrespects the body" to that of Mellors, the gamekeeper, who believes in the "touch of bodily awareness". Mellors and Cannie Chatterley together herald the brave new world that Lawrence believed in and hoped for. "The human body is only just coming to real life. With the Greeks it gave a lovely flicker, then Plato and Aristotle killed it, and Jesus finished it off. But now the body is coming really to life; it is really rising from the tomb. And it will be a lovely, lovely life in the lovely universe, the life of the human body" (p. 274).

The process of making friends with the black horse, of discovering the body and coming to terms with it, is seen to be more complex in *Women in Love.* While in *Lady Chatterley's Lover* the contrast between Clifford and his cronies on the one hand who look upon the body as an adjunct and a disability and Mellors and Connie who believe in the "touch of bodily awareness" on the other is neat and striking, the two pairs of lovers in *Women in Love* cannot be so easily distinguished.

Talking about the positive values—'the norms for the relations of man and woman in marriage'. F. R. Leavis writes:

> But the need of some norm for the relations between men and women other than what Gerald and Gudrun enact is cogently presented by the 'tale'. Birkin posits a relation that shall be in its vitality, stable and

> permanent because the terms between which it subsists are real; the need or demand of neither of the two individuals who find fulfilment in the relation is of such a kind as to deny the individual being of the one or of the other.[7]

For Mark Spilka the positives are Blutbruderschaft and star-equilibrium. In his 'Introduction' to *D. H. Lawrence: Twentieth Century Views,* he observes:

> If Lawrence makes an impressive indictment of the modern wasteland, he does so through his engagement with neglected values or new possibilities of value, like Blutbruderschaft and 'Star-equilibrium'.[8]

I believe the positives are localized elsewhere. To be sure, Lawrence had a horror of merging and mingling that romantic love implied. It becomes his obsessive concern in *Aaron's Rod,* and the same is reflected in Birkin's relationship with Ursula. Also, Birkin is constantly talking about 'Star-equilibrium' and *Blutbruderschaft*—the first only expressing in a graphic manner Lawrence's concern for separateness and the second at best remains a subsidiary theme in *Women in Love.*[9] But what is central to *Women in Love* is not star-equilibrium, nor Blutbruderschaft but the unself-conscious acceptance of the erotic and the aggressive on the part of Birkin and Ursula—the coming to terms with the dark-self. It is this that distinguishes them from Gerald and Gudrun and makes for wholeness of being and freedom.

Both Gudrun and Gerald lack the capacity to strip themselves of ego and personality and become "two stark, unknown beings, two utterly strange creatures", while Ursula and Birkin come to each other "without reserves or defences, stripped entirely, into the unknown". A reading of the two chapters 'Excurse' and 'Death and Love' together will clearly establish the point. While the deliberate, mental nature of Gerald-Gudrun affair, analysed at length in the last chapter. is suggested by the image "like Eve reaching to the apples on the tree of knowledge", the experience that Birkin and Ursula undergo is altogether of a different kind. While the former may be called postlapsarian, the latter is prelapsarian. "She saw a strange creature from another world in him. It was as if she were enchanted, and everything were metamorphosed. She recalled again the old magic of the Book of

Genesis, where the Sons of God saw the daughters of men, that they were fair. And he was one of these, one of these strange creatures from the beyond looking down at her, and seeing she was fair" (p. 352). It must be admitted, however, that Lawrence's success here in not as complete as in 'Death and Love', but the intent is unmistakable. Lawrence is positing the "unspeakable communication in touch", the "vital sensual reality that can never be transmuted into mind content" against the deliberate, mental knowing to gratify one's ego as in the case of Gerald and Gudrun.

Similarly, while a certain amount of aggression marks the relationships of both Gerald-Gudrun and Birkin-Ursula, there is a basic difference. As suggested earlier the conflict between Gerald and Gudrun is essentially a cold war. Birkin and Ursula, on the other hand, fight a no-holds-barred hot war to preserve the impersonal third thing. Ursula's assault on Birkin is motivated by her feeling that Birkin lacks the courage to altogether break with the dead past, while Gudrun's attacks on Gerald are like clever moves in a game meant to preserve her autonomy. Compare, for example:

> 'What are your plans for tomorrow?' She asked nonchalantly whilst her heart was beating so furiously.
>
> If he sees it I'm done for forever—you know you're done for forever, if he sees the absurd state you're in?' (p. 466)
>
> And,
>
> Suddenly a flame ran over her, and she stamped her foot madly on the road.
>
> 'And I, I'm not spiritual enough, I'm not as spiritual as that Hermione?' (p. 345)

In the case of Gudrun, there is a split between the conscious and the unconscious: the assumed non-chalance of "what are your plans for tomorrow" is meant to conceal her inner agitation, and her prime concern is not to give herself away. By contrast, Ursula's indignation springs from the roots of her being and engages her total self. So while Gerald and Gudrun manipulate erotic and aggressive impulses for mental gratification or egoistic assetion, Birkin and Ursula accept them in their own right and achieve wholeness of being.

Birkin-Ursula quarrel serves a therapeutic purpose burning them into essentiality and paving the way for profound sensual communion. It is significant that Birkin does not go to see Hermione; instead they both drive to Sherwood Forest. The cold-blooded conflict between Gerald and Gudrun alienates them further ending in the death of Gerald in the Alpine snows.

Again, it is Lawrence's concern for wholeness and sanity that accounts for his acceptance of the bestial and the so-called perverse. In his essay "Reality of Peace" Lawrence observes:

> If there is a serpent of secret and shameful desire in my soul, let me not beat it out of my consciousness with sticks. It will be beyond, in the marsh of the so-called subconsciousness, where I cannot follow it with my sticks. Let me bring it to the fire to see what it is. For a serpent is a thing created. It has its own *raison d'etre.* In its own being it has beauty and reality. Even my horror is a tribute to its reality. And I must admit the genuineness of my horror, accept it, and not exclude it from my understanding. . . . But may be my understanding will drain the swampy place and the serpent will evaporate as his condition evaporates.[10]

Laurentian protagonists like Ursula in *Women in Love* and Connie Chatterley in *Lady Chatterley's Lover* seem to uphold this view: to achieve wholeness and freedom by inclusion, not exclusion. For example, Ursula observing "the sardonic licentious mockery of his (Birkin's) eyes" first recoils in horror and then accepts it as a part of the whole. "Why not be bestial, and go the whole round of experience? She exulted in it. She was bestial. How good it was to be really shameful! There would be no shameful things she had not experienced. Yet she was unabashed, she was herself. Why not? She was free, when she knew everything, and no dark shameful things were denied her" (p. 464). Connie undergoes a similar experience in *Lady Chatterley's Lover.* The "sensual fire" burns out shame, and she becomes a freer person. "There was nothing left to disguise or be ashamed of. She shared her ultimate nakedness with a man, another being" (p. 289).

Lawrence's use of dialect and four-letter words must also be seen as a part of his endeavour to make friends with the black horse—to recognize the separateness and autonomy of the passional self which exists prior to and independent of mental consciousness. (Significantly, the second version of *Lady Chatterley's Lover* is called *John Thomas and Lady Jane.*) This necessitates a different language from the one employed by men like Clifford who view everything through the prism of anthropocentric consciousness. Barbara Hardy makes an extremely perceptive observation in *The Appropriate Form:*

> The obscenities are the linguistic antithesis to the readymade literary language which comes between her (Connie) and life. The language which Mellors teaches her is also new to her, not readymade. Its rough naming of life is at the opposite pole from Sir Clifford's unresponsive use of literary language, its outrageousness functions like grim satire. The flowers she gives to Mellors are used in their love-making, and when Mellors observes 'Pretty as life', the natural equation is plainly made, and the antithesis completed.[11]

"The readymade literary language" employed by Clifford denies life. For him "violets are Juno's eyelids". Connie is repelled by this, for she sees in it the complacency and arrogance of anthropocentric consciousness—an attempt to absorb the strange otherness of flowers to one's own mentality. Mellors is Clifford's antithesis; for him flowers are pretty because they are alive, not because they approximate literary descriptions.

Similarly, Lawrence's use of four-letter words is part of his battle against the Platonic-Christian degrading of the body. For 'dirty' words are of a piece with the Phaedrus mentality, of splitting life into two halves—the spiritual and the physical—and identifying the essential with the former. How Lawrence tries to deprive the four-letter words of their 'dirty' connotations and make us accept them as natural is best illustrated by Constance Chatterley's conversation with the gamekeeper in *The First Lady Chatterley:*

> 'What do you call me in your sort of talk?'
>
> 'My Lover!' she stammered. 'Lover!' he re-echoed. A queer flash went over his face.
>
> 'Fucker!' he said, and his eyes darted a flash at her, as if he shot her.
>
> The word, she knew from Clifford, was obsence, and she flushed deeply and then went pale. But since the word itself had so little association to her, it made very little impression on her. . . .
>
> 'But,' she stammered, 'even if you are—are you ashamed of it?'

> He had been looking at her curiously, watchfully, like a dog that has bitten somebody. His expression slowly changed to one of perplexed doubt.
>
> 'Am I ashamed of it?' he questioned vaguely.
>
> 'Yes! Even if you are my "fucker" as you call it, are you ashamed of it? There is nothing to be ashamed of in it, is there.' (p. 127)

"Fucker" is a 'dirty' word. Parkings utters it with a certain amount of savage contempt thinking it would hurt her. The "diabolic hate" gives way to perplexed doubt when he sees it has made no impression on her. And when she comes with the poser, "Even if you are my 'fucker' as you call it, are you ashamed of it?" his moral prejudices fall off and he seems to see without the prism of civilized consciousness which degrades the sex act and the female partner engaged in the act.

From love of woman to the living contact with the non-human universe is the next step. In fact, the two are intimately connected, for "it is the penis which connects us sensually with the planets. But for the penis we should never know the loveliness of sirius or the categorical difference between a pomegranate and an India-rubber ball." (*The First Lady Chatterley*, p. 156)

It is not an accident that only characters like Ursula, Connie and Mellors—characters who have the capacity to establish a passional relationship with a man or a woman—reveal a living awareness of the non-human world. Others like Gerald, Gudrun and Clifford are cut off from it by their will or mentality which commits them totally to the man-made world. To live with the cosmos and know it as greater than oneself is to experience wonder and mystery—the wonder and mystery men in the pagan phase had always known and the moderns have lost. In *Apocalypse* Lawrence observes:

> Perhaps the greatest difference between us and the pagans lies in our different relation to the cosmos. With us, all is personal. Landscape and the sky, these are to us the delicious background of our personal life, and no more. Even the universe of the *scientist* is little more than an extension of our personality, to us. To the pagan, landscape and personal background were on the whole indifferent. But the cosmos was a very real thing. A man *lived* with the cosmos and knew it greater than himself.[12]

A living non-mental awareness of the cosmos permeates all Lawrence's fiction. The intimate moments between Paul and Clara, for instance, acquire a greater significance when they include "in their meeting the thrust of the manifold grass-stems, the cry of the peewit, the wheel of the stars" (p. 430). Ursula is *The Rainbow*, knows that "the light of science and knowledge" was "like the area under an arc-lamp" which fenced out the "grey shadow-shapes of wild-beasts", and also the "dark shadow-shapes of the angels" (p. 438). Similarly, Birkin in *Women in Love* finds his contact with the primroses rejuvenating after the negative encounter with Hermione. However, it is in Lawrence's short story "Sun" and the novella "St. Mawr" that we have non-human protagonists, which are of special relevance to the present discussion.

"Sun" is about Juliet's relationship with the sun. The sun is the leading protagonist. Lawrence does not anthropomorphize it, and to make the sun symbolic of something human is to kill the story. Mark Spilka in his book *The Love Ethic of D. H. Lawrence* insists on the literal nature of his symbolism, and disapproves of Tindall's symbolic interpretation. "The story stands or falls on the woman's living contact with the sun. The connection is organic and dramatic, and what Tindall really finds odd here is the thought that man can live in anything but an alien universe."[13]

I believe Spilka is right, for the essential point of the story seems to be that the modern civilized existence divorced from the non-human is diseased, and it is this disease that Juliet sheds when she responds to the sun. Juliet is an ailing woman. She needs the sun; like all civilized creatures she is suffering from sun-deficiency. Her ailment is shown in her irritability and her sickening sense of responsibility. "The child irritated her, and preyed on her peace of mind. She felt so horribly, ghastly responsible for him: as if she must be responsible for every breath he drew"[14] (p. 28).

The sun is the cosmic, non-human lover she initially resists. "He faced down to her with his look of blue fire, and enveloped her breasts and her face, her throat, her tired belly, her knees, her thighs and her feet" (p. 29). She is completely transformed by her contact with the sun. She is freed from 'anxious love-anguish' and fretting, and develops a certain amount of insouciance:

> 'Bring me the orange,' she said amazed at her own deep indifference to his trepidation. 'Bring Mummy the orange.'
>
> 'He shall not grow up like his father,' she said to herself 'like a worm that the sun has never seen.' (p. 31)

The Italian peasant Juliet wants to meet would be 'a procreative sunbath'. The peasant is a human manifestation of the sun, not vice versa.

With "St. Mawr" we have moved a long way from the standard English novel with its bourgeois hero, for the protagonist here is a horse. The chief characters like Lou, Rico and Phoenix etc. are defined in terms of their attitude to St. Mawr. To interpret the novella entirely in humanistic terms, as F. R. Leavis does, is surely to limit its meaning. To quote Leavis:

> By 'body', then, Lawrence means all that deep spontaneous life which is not at the back and call of the conscious and willing mind, and so in that sense cannot be controlled by it, though it can be thwarted and defeated. St. Mawr, the stallion, is that life. And in presenting the drama in which the stallion figures so centrally Lawrence leaves us unable to doubt that his essential concern is to vindicate 'love, joy, delight, hope, true indignant anger, passionate sense of justice and injustice, truth and untruth, honour and dishonour', and the capacity for real belief.[15]

Mark Spilka's remark about the symbolism of Lawrence referred to earlier is instructive, for St. Mawr is not just a phallic symbol, not merely the repressed or thwarted consciousness. Leavis, I am afraid, does not show adequate appreciation of the non-human dimension and chooses to read it as a 'human' tale vindicating 'love, joy, delight. . . .' St. Mawr is in the first place a horse—the non-human locus of mystery and wonder of existence that the categories of rational humanism cannot parcel. To reduce it altogether to a human symbol is to commit the sin of humanistic culture—the sin that Rico commits when he dismisses the horse as 'marvellous colour'. This is precisely the point of Lou's response to St. Mawr. To know St. Mawr, as Lou does, is to be aware of the poverty of the human all-too-human existence.

As the novella progresses, one becomes aware that Lou's encounter with St. Mawr had larger implications, that the choice between an effete, arty-arty Rico and a splendid, dangerous animal is in fact a choice between a safe, dangerless man-centred civilization and a dangerous, wonderful world where men live in close proximity with 'equine twilight'. And Lou chooses the latter, for she cannot live without wonder. ". . . I want the wonder back again, or I shall die." And St. Mawr is the sole embodiment of the non-human wonder, the wholeness that men ruled by will and sundered from the non-human seem incapable of. "He seems a far greater mystery to me than a clever man, He's a horse. Why can't one say in the same way, of a man: He's a man? There seems no mystery in being a man. But there is a terrible mystery in St. Mawr" (p. 55).

Also, the battlelines are clearly drawn between Rico, the Manbys and the Dean who want the horse shot and Low, Phoenix and Lewis who would like to save it, between those who want a safe, dangerless, man-centered world and those who would like to live in vital contact with Pan, for there is no wonder in a man-made world and they die without wonder. The anthropocentric arrogance of the 'civilized' man comes out clearly in the sarcastic rejoinder of the Dean:

> 'Mrs Witt, you are playing on words.'
>
> 'No, Dean Vyner, I am not. My son-in-law pulled that horse over backwards and pinned him down with the reins.'
>
> 'I am sorry for the horse,' said the Dean with heavy sarcasm. (p. 90)

The 'intolerance' of the civilized Dean is in striking contrast to Phoenix's recognition of the otherness of the horse:

> 'Don't you like St. Mawr, Phoenix?'
>
> 'I like him. He is a very good horse.'
>
> 'Even after what he's done to Sir Henry?'
>
> 'That don't make no difference to him being a good horse?'
>
> 'But suppose he had done it to you?'
>
> 'I don't care, I say it my own fault.' (p. 84)

To sum up, "the tremendous non-human quality of life" is the key to Laurentian vision of a "greater society". It means repudiating the exclusiveness of the Christian ideal and accepting love in its wholeness—even the so-called bestial and perverse without shame or guilt. Also, it implies a non-mental, living relationship with the circumambient universe as in Juliet's contact with the sun and Lou's encounter with the horse, for "to live with the cosmos and know it greater than oneself" is to experience wonder and mystery and escape the prison of anthropocentric consciousness.

NOTES AND REFERENCES

1. "Vivas tends to efface or neutralise every positive value in Lawrence, and to accept him only as a maker of wasteland novels." Mark Spilka, *D. H. Lawrence: Twentieth Century Views,* p. 10.
2. The letters of D. H. Lawrence, ed. George J. Zytaruk and James T. Boulton (Cambridge: Cambridge University Press, 1981), II, p. 218.

   Also, in her biography of Lawrence, Brenda Maddox observes, "The expressionless of the Indians made a deep impression on him. 'Mindlers, without effort . . . they dance on and on'. Their ritual stirred ideas latent since his college Botany days: that man was just part of the great pageant of Nature in which the inanimate held equal place with the animate." *The Married Man—A Life of D. H. Lawrence.*
3. D. H. Lawrence, "A Propos of Lady Chatterley's Lover", *A Selection from Phoenix,* ed. A.A.H. Inglis (Harmondsworth: Penguin, 1979), p. 353.
4. The Phaedrus myth makes its appearance again in *John Thomas and Lady Jane* the second version of *Lady Chatterley's Lover.* Here too Constance, while talking to Clifford, expresses her disapproval of Socrates' treatment of the black horse in unequivocal terms: "I do think Socrates seems awfully stupid and overbearing with his black horse." (p. 88)

   However, there is no reference to the Phaedrus myth in the third version.
5. *Appropriate Form* (1964; rpt. London: Athlone Press, 1971), p. 155.
6. Lawrence once wrote to Rosalind Baynes the woman who in all probability inspired his portrayal of Constance Chatterley: "Let us think of love as a force outside and getting us. It is a force; a god. The ancients had it and for them there were no personalisms and they were men and still had pride."

   Cited in Brenda Maddox's *The Married Man—A Life of D. H. Lawrence,* p. 280.
7. *D. H. Lawrence: Novelist,* p. 215.
8. *D. H. Lawrence: Twentieth Century Views,* p. 10.
9. The theme of blood-brotherhood disappears altogether in *Lady Chatterley's Lover.* It does figure prominently in *Aaron's Red, Kangaroo* and *The Plumed*

Serpent, but its value seems to be at least partly biographical. Lawrence is setting up man-man relationship as a counterweight against the power of the domineering female. Anyway, it would be on one's case that Lawrence is at his creative best in those works.

10. *Phoenix: The Posthumous Papers of D. H. Lawrence*, p. 677–78.
11. *The Appropriate Form,* p. 165.
12. *Apocalypse*, p. 27.
13. *The Love Ethic of D. H. Lawrence* (London: Dennis Dobson, 1958), p. 42.
14. *Sun* in *The Woman Who Rode Away and Other Stories*, Harmondsworth: Penguin, 1950.
15. *D. H. Lawrence: Novelist*, p. 279.

Chapter 6

BRONTË, LAWRENCE AND THE 'CARBON'

IN HIS MONUMENTAL *History of English Literature*, Hippolyte Taine observes:

> A character is a force, like gravity, or steam . . . which must be defined otherwise than by the amount of weight it can lift or the havoc it can cause. It is, therefore, to ignore man, to reduce him . . . to make him an aggregate of virtues and vices; it is to lose sight in him of all but the exterior and social side; it is to neglect the inner and natural element. We will find the same fault in English criticism, always moral, never psychological . . . we will find the same fault in English religion, which is but an emotion or a discipline; in their philosophy, destitute of metaphysics; and if we ascend to the source . . . we will see all these weaknesses derived from their native energy, their practical education, and that kind of severe and religious poetic instinct which has in time past made them Protestant and Puritan.[1]

Taine's observation seems to be a shrewd assessment of the English sensibility—at any rate as it manifests itself in fiction. Spilka quoting Taine with implicit approval calls Lawrence "the first English novelist to explore man's natural elements".[2] My contention is Lawrence is not the first English novelist to do so and Taine's observation does not hold true of Emily Brontë's *Wuthering Heights*, for here is a novel which is concerned centrally with "the inner and natural element" and not with "the exterior and social side"—the staple concern of British fiction. The point I wish to make here is that Emily Brontë is pre-eminently D. H. Lawrence's precursor,[3] and *Wuthering Heights* the sort of novel Lawrence believed he was writing for the first time as he claimed in his oft-quoted letter to Edward Garnett:

> . . . that which is physic—non-human, in humanity, is more interesting to me than the old-fashioned human element—which causes one to conceive a character in a certain moral scheme and make him consistent.

> The certain moral scheme is what I object to . . . when Marinetti writes: "It is the solidity of a blade of steel that is interesting by itself, that is, the incomprehending and inhuman alliance of its molecules in resistance to let us say, bullet, the heat of a piece of wood, or iron is in fact more passionate, for us, than the laughter or tears of a woman"—then I know what he means. He is stupid as an artist, for contrasting the heat of the iron and the laughter of the woman. Because what is interesting in the laughter of the woman is the same as the binding of the molecular of steel or their action in heat; it is the inhuman will, call it physiology, or like Marinetti—the physiology of matter, that fascinates me. I don't so much care about what the woman feels—in the ordinary usage of the word. That presumes an ego to feel with. I only care about what the woman is what she is—inhumanly, physiologically, materially—according to the use of the word: but for me what she is as a phenomenon (or as representing some greater inhuman will), instead of what she feels according to the human conception. . . . You mustn't look in my novel for the old stable ego of the character. There is another ego, according to whose action the individual is unrecognisable, and passes through, as it were, allotropic states which it needs a deeper sense than any we have been used to discover are states of the same single radically unchanged element. (Like as diamond and coal are the same pure single elements of carbon. The ordinary novel would trace the history of the diamond—but I say, "Diamond, what! And my diamond might be coal or soot, and my theme is carbon'.)[4]

Lawrence's letter—his manifesto as it were—could serve as an equally appropriate description of Brontë's aims as a novelist, for she is as much concerned with the "non-human in humanity" as Lawrence. In fact, what unites the two and distinguishes them from the rest of the tribe is their interest in the non-human. Admittedly, Lawrence himself viewed Hardy as his precursor à la study of Thomas Hardy. It seems to me, however, that Hardy is too burdened with mind-consciousness to explore the 'carbon'. His protagonists are nearly crippled by the consciousness of an indifferent or hostile fate and hence have a "weak life-flow". Brontë's protagonists are far more "explosive" and therefore true kindred spirits of an Ursula Brangwen, a Rupert Birkin or a Constance Chatterley. Brontë, like Lawrence, is not interested in the history of the diamond; her theme too is carbon—the "single radically unchanged element". The Brontë-Lawrence rejection—in Brontë's care perhaps an unconscious one—of the old novel of character is rooted in the intuition that the human self is not to be equated with ego, that life is prior to and larger than will and conciousness and that the roots of man's being are in nature. (It is significant that animal imagery abounds in their fiction.) Characters in Brontë and D. H. Lawrence are constantly forgetting their manners and getting off the moral groove. Stripped of their humanity, they become primal forces like a torrent or an earthquake. Catherine Earnshaw may truly be called the precursor of the Laurentian heroine; she is a Nietzschean immoralist in the same sense as the latter is.[5] "I only care for what the woman is—inhumanly, physiologically, materially." This is as true of Catherine Earnshaw as of Ursula Brangwen. It is amazing indeed that with the exception of Keith Sagar few critics have noticed this central affinity between Lawrence and Brontë.[6] No doubt, this is partly, at least, owing to Leavis's curious dismissal of *Wuthering Heights* as "a literary sport". K. Sagar, however, recognizes this affinity in his book, *The Art of D. H. Lawrence* though he makes just a passing reference to it. "Emily Brontë and Lawrence both care less about analysing what a woman feels than about grasping what she is.'[7]

Later, in his essay on "The Originality of Wuthering Heights", Sagar clearly underlines Emily Brontë's significance as a precursor of D. H. Lawrence:

> In any case, it is not true that *Wuthering Heights* is a sport, only that it belongs to a much older and less limiting tradition than that of the English realistic novel of the late 18th and 19th centuries. Behind her is certainly Shakespeare—what novel is closer to Macbeth or King Lear? Ahead of her is the *Heart of Darkness, The Rainbow, Women in Love, St. Mawr.*[8]

Sagar, however, restricts himself to observations of a general nature, and fails to appreciate the full extent of their affinities. "The work of Lawrence's which most strongly suggests itself for direct comparison is not a work of fiction at all, but the poem, 'Snake'."[9] The following discussion, I hope, would establish that the 'direct comparison' of Lawrence's fiction with that of Brontë is valid and fruitful, for the affinities between the two are deeper than Sagar imagines.

In *Wuthering Heights* Heathcliff, to use the terminology of Lawrence's letter, is pure "carbon". He is a primal force rather than a character, having escaped the humanizing process altogether first because of Hindley's tyranny and later out of his own choosing. One hardly thinks of him as a human being. He seems to have more in common with his dogs than with the people he encounters. Even Catherine with whom he has a deep affinity—a sort of blood sympathy—describes him as "a fierce, pitiless, wolfish man". His analogues in fiction are Moby Dick the white whale in Melville's classic and St. Mawr the fiery stallion in Lawrence's novella.

But is he so very different from other people? Is Emily Brontë not trying to demonstrate that there is a Heathcliff in all civilized beings? For Heathcliff performs the role of a catalytic agent; and those who come in contact with him are stripped of their humanity, their societal self and become 'essential' beings. In Lawrence's terminology, the contact with Heathcliff burns the diamond of consciousness, of secondary civilized self and brings forth the carbon of the primal self. Isabella is its most outstanding example; she is Heathcliff's most important victim. The shocking discovery that Heathcliff has married her solely to gain power over her brother and use her as a lever against him turns her infatuated admiration into savage hatred. She becomes so imbued with the Heathcliff spirit that if certain lines are lifted out of context, it would be difficult to identify their speaker.

> 'I would rather he suffered *less* if I might cause his sufferings and he might *know* that I was the cause. Oh, I owe him so much. On only one condition can I hope to forgive him. It is, if I may take an eye for an eye, a tooth for a tooth; for every wrench of agony return a wrench; reduce him to my level.' (p. 215)

Here is Isabella Linton, the civilized lady from Thrushcross Grange, enunciating the unchristian maxim "an eye for an eye, a tooth for a tooth". And when Nelly Dean scolds her for her unchristian conduct, her rejoinder is strongly reminiscent of Heathcliff's earlier in the novel when he declares his resolve to take revenge on Hindlay:

> 'Fie, fie, Miss!' I interrupted. 'One might suppose you had never opened a Bible in your life. If God afflict your enemies, surely that ought to suffice you. It is both mean and presumptuous to add your torture to his!'
>
> 'In general, I'll allow that it would be Ellen,' she continued, 'but that misery laid on Heathcliff would content me, unless I have a hand in it?' (p. 215)

Heathcliff had reacted similarly to Nelly Dean's sermonizing:

> 'For shame, Heathcliff!' said I. 'It is for God to punish wicked people. We should learn to forgive.' 'No, God won't have the satisfaction that I shall,' he returned. (p. 101)

Even Catherine Linton who boasts of a "better nature" and prides herself on her tolerance and magnanimity is delighted by the feeling that Heathcliff's cruelly arises from his greater misery:

> 'Mr. Heathcliff, *you* have *nobody* to love you, and however miserable you make us, we shall still have the revenge of thinking that your cruelty arises from your greater misery! You are miserable, are you not? Lonely, like the devil, and envious like him? *Nobody* loves you—nobody will cry for you when you die! I wouldn't be you!' (p. 319)

Also, we have it from Nelly Dean that Edgar Linton abhorred Heathcliff with an intensity which the mildness of his nature would scarcely seem to allow. So the encounter with Heathcliff reduces even the most civilized of them to their animal 'essence'. Emily Brontë thus demonstrates that under our civilized skin we are naked, and also the utter inadequacy of Christian ideals in the face of existential questions.

Lawrence shares Brontë's central perception that the civilized man is a dressed-up creature, and his fiction too is concerned with the stripping of the societal, and the discovery of the primal. Constance Chatterley seems to speak for the author when she observes in *The First Lady Chatterley:*

> One thing she clearly saw: that human nature, under all its dead surface of habit is, like the earth, volcanic and will inevitably start to upheave one day, when the pressure from within is too great or there is a call from the outside. (p. 78)

It is "human nature" under "its dead surface of habit" Lawrence is concerned with, and it is this element that he means by the term "carbon". The imagery employed to describe Constance's metamorphosis ("This starting of the whole being, body and soul and mind, in a new flux that would change one away from the old self as a landscape is transfigured by earthquake and lava floods, or by spring and the coming of summer") recalls Lawrence's observation is the Garnett letter: "I only care about what the woman is—what she is—inhumanly, physiologically, materially . . . what she is as a phenomenon." He is not interested in Lady Chatterley the elegant hostess of Wragby but the strange woman "so soft and boundless and gentle but also remorseless like the sea" (p. 78). The Lawrence protagonist comes to realize the grave limitation of "extant consciousness"—the-manners-and-morals world—when it comes to existential issues. Lou Witt in "St. Mawr" undergoes a similar experience though in her case the awakening from the secondary self is brought about by the stallion: "Looming like some good out of the darkness was the head of that horse, with the wide, terrible questioning eyes. And she felt that it forbade her to be just Rico's wife, young Lady Carrington and all that" (p. 22).

This realization—what one may call "carbon"-consciousness (à la the Garnett letter)—is not, however, confined to marvellous metamorphoses alone; it expresses itself in day-to-day conflict. In *Women in Love*, for instance, there are no marvellous changes; it is the conflict, the hot war between friends and also between lovers, that serves as a process of sifting the social husk from the primal kernel. A Laurentian quarrel is a dramatic encounter where human beings strip themselves of their societal personalities, set aside the notions of decency and propriety and engage in an intimate, if fierce, communion. Quarrels occupy a crucial place in *Women in Love*. First, we shall discuss the quarrels between Birkin and Hermione (Classroom), between Ursula and Hermione (Woman to Woman) and finally turn to the one between Birkin and Ursula (Excurse).

To start with the quarrel between Birkin and Hermione, one might find the savagery and nastiness of Birkin's attack on Hermione revolting if one comes to Lawrence with the attitude associated with the traditional English novel. But this would be misreading the novel and doing Lawrence great injustice. For what we have her is not the clash of personalities, but that of impersonal forces. It is not that Birkin has ceased to be a person, a human being. Birkin's feelings even at the given moment are complicated. They are a complex of hate and contempt and shame, and above all "a bitter red anger" (p. 46). Birkin is aware of the fact he is hurting Hermione; he is even ashamed of doing so, but the ruling passion is "a bitterer red anger" which makes him a "passionate voice". And this "red anger" is directed not at Hermione personally; it is directed at someone who embodies "the worst and last form of intellectualism." It is interesting that the reaction of Ursula to the brutal spectacle is not in conventional terms. She does not feel sorry for Hermione nor is she repelled by Birkin's harsh treatment. Significantly, Ursula is described as turning "pale and abstracted".

Later, Ursula's quarrel with Hermione (Woman to Woman) is set in the same key where the diplomatic barbs of the elegant Hermione provoke Ursula to launch a characteristically frontal assault on the former. Ursula, of course, is peeved by Hermione's suggestion that she is merely a "physical woman", but her attack on Hermione is not primarily inspired by jealousy. She is attacking the lie that is Hermione. She flings aside all decency and propriety, forgets her manners and attacks Hermione brutally. "What is the good of your talking about love—you untrue spectre of a woman! How can you know anything, when you don't believe? You don't believe in yourself and your own womanhood, so what good is your conceited, shallow cleverness—!" (p. 334).

Hermione remains the cool, superior intellectual female, ignoring the 'brainless', emotional Ursula. But she is not just the supercilious, aristocratic female of the standard English novel. The characteristic Laurentian perspective on her is provided in the very beginning of the novel where she is shown to be "vulnerable" and "in spite of all her vanity and security, any common maid-servant of positive, robust temper could fling down this bottomless pit of insufficiency, with the slightest movement of jeering or contempt!" (p. 18). Significantly, her "aesthetic knowledge and culture, and world-visions, and disinterestedness" cannot fence out the animal as is seen in her trying to biff Birkin.

The most significant, however, is the lovers' quarrel—the one between Birkin and Ursula, and it is this I shall now examine along with the quarrel between Heathcliff and Catherine in *Wuthering Heights* (Chapter 15).

Lawrence is generally taken to be the first English novelist to have perceived that man-woman relationship is a more complex affair than the romantic or idealistic notions of love would permit. Barbara Hardy, for instance, observes, "One of his most important contributions to the realism of fiction, in theory and in practice, in his rejection of the kind of specialized emotion which is the basis of the Victorian novel and of many twentieth century delineations of love. In the Victorian novel, you are either in love or not, it is an absolute state . . ."[10]

It is my contention that in Brontë, Lawrence has a precursor and that the relation between Catherine and Heathcliff shows a similar multiplicity of emotion. As the present discussion would show, for Brontë, as for Lawrence, love is a complex, even impure, emotion made of passion and anger and also tenderness.

The lovers' quarrels in *Wuthering Heights* and *Women in Love* are the finest example of what Lawrence calls "carbon" in his Garnett letter. In the first place, no attempt is made by the characters involved to keep the conflict within the bounds of propriety or decency. The quarrels—and it is as true of the Catherine-Heathcliff quarrel as of the one between Birkin and Ursula—are in the nature of a hot-war, an all-out, no-holds-barred affair. Also, they are marked by an honesty which can only be called brutal, impelled as they are by the desire to speak the bitter stark truth involving a total eschewing of illusion and idealization.[11]

Compare for instance:

> 'Are you possessed with a devil,' he pursued, savagely, 'to talk in that manner to me when you are dying? Do you reflect that all those words will be branded in my memory, and eating deeper eternally after you have left me? You know you lie to say I have killed you and Catherine, you know that I could as soon forget you as my existence! Is it not sufficient for your infernal selfishness, that while you are at peace, I shall writhe in the torments of hell?' (*Wuthering Heights*, p. 196)

And,

> 'No, it's you who are a liar. It's you who must return, like a dog to his vomit. It is what Hermione *stands* for that I hate. I hate it. It is lies, it is false, it is death. But you want it, you can't help it, you can't help yourself. You belong to that old, deathly way of living—then go back to it. But don't come to me, for I have nothing to do with it?' (*Women in Love*, p. 348)

Secondly, the protagonists involved cease to be persons and become primal forces. The open and all-out conflict strips them of their ego and their consciousness. This is true of Heathcliff and Ursula to a larger extent than of Birkin and Catherine. Compare,

> He flung hurriedly into the nearest seat, and on my approaching timidly to ascertain if she had fainted, he gnashed at me, and foamed like a mad dog, and gathered her to him with greedy jealousy. I did not feel as I were in the company of a creature of my own species. . . . (*Wuthering Heights*, p. 197)

and,

> Suddenly, a flame ran over her, and she stamped her foot madly on the road, and he winced, afraid that she would strike him. 'And I, I'm not spiritual enough, I'm not as spiritual as that Hermione—'. Her brows knitted, her eyes blazed like a tiger's. (*Women in Love*, p. 345)

Heathcliff foams "like a mad dog", Ursula's eyes blaze like a "tiger's". Ursula stamps her foot "madly on the road" and Birkin is afraid that she would strike him. Nelly is so awed by Heathcliff's mad passion that she thinks she was not in the company of a creature of her own species. The invasion of personality by the Dionysian—the non-human—is appropriately conveyed by the use of animal imagery.

There is an important difference, however. Although quarrels serve a therapeutic function in both Brontë and Lawrence, they are differently structured. The aggressive and erotic emotions in Lawrence are sequentially related, while in Brontë they seem to exist simultaneously. For example, the prelapsarian meeting between Ursula and Birkin *follows* a cleansing operation. Ursula must demolish the "salvator mundi" in Birkin in order to find in him a Son of God. Significantly, the "ugly, malevolent look" yields to the "wonderful yellow light" when she has murdered the preacher in Birkin and thus in the process murdered her own hatred of him. In *Wuthering Heights* passion and rage and even tenderness are intimately blended. Anger and hatred form as much a part of the Catherine-Heathcliff relations as tears and kisses. And what makes for the intensity, and power of the last meeting between them is the subtle movement from passion to anger, and from anger to tenderness. Heathcliff kisses Catherine frantically immediately after he enters her room. "He bestowed more kisses than even he gave in his life before" (p. 194). . . . A little later he accuses her savagely of "infernal selfishness". And when Catherine asks him to come near her, he would not let her see his face "which was livid with emotion". Thus, Heathcliff kisses and burns and rages at the same time making his life "a rainbow of love and hate"[12] something that perhaps no other British novelist did before D. H. Lawrence.

The 'madness' of the Brontë and Lawrence protagonists then stems from the fidelity to their demon, from their desire to preserve the "carbon" without which there can be no authentic selfhood. The problem for the Brontë, as also for the Lawrence, protagonist is how to preserve the carbon—the affective self from the deadening abstractions of 'society' and 'culture'. It inevitably brings them into clash with the prevailing norms and values and makes them—Catherine and Heathcliff as much as Ursula and Constance and Mellors—at once vulnerable and cruel. They are vulnerable in a sense that the 'civilized' ones like Clifford, Rico and Lockwood are not. They can be hurt vitally as Lockwood and Clifford cannot be, for the latter have either shut off the primal self altogether (e.g. Lockwood, Clifford Chatterley) or with the help of categorical imperatives, to modify a Nietzschean formulation, have "moderated or debilitated their primal impulses" as in the case of Edgar. We may recall Heathcliff's 'mad' outburst on Catherine's death, and compare it with Edgar's 'sane' acceptance of it.

Similarly, in *Lady Chatterley's Lover* while Hilda makes herself invulnerable by winning her "freedom", by keeping off men, Connie (Constance in *First Lady Chatterley*) has the vulnerability of living things. For to live is to connect, to enter into relationships and thus become vulnerable. "Poor thing, she too had some of the vulnerability of the wild hyacinths, she wasn't all tough rubber goods and platinum like the modern girl" (p. 136).

Admittedly, the vulnerability of Heathcliff is not the same thing as that of Connie and the metaphors employed by the novelists make it amply clear. Heathcliff is likened to a savage beast while Connie is like the wild hyacinths. While Heathcliff's passion is marked by fierceness, Connie's is a tender thing. Still they both belong to the organic, wild reality as distinguished from a civilized existence made possible by insentience or moderation.

The cruelty of the Brontë and Lawrence protagonists must be seen as a necessary condition of living; their fidelity to the self, as suggested earlier, inevitably brings them into clash with the categorical imperatives and the persons who embody them.

Catherine's passionate welcome to Heathcliff when he returns after a long absence may be cruel from a moralistic angle for it mortifies Edgar, yet given Catherine's nature it is inevitable. "They were too much absorbed in their mutual joy to suffer embarrassment; not so Mr. Edgar, he grew pale with pure annoyance, a feeling that reached its climax when his lady rose and stepping across the rug, seized Heathcliff's hands again, and laughed like one besides herself" (p. 135–36).

Constance's resolve to leave Clifford in *First Lady Chatterley* is equally 'cruel', but not to desert Clifford would amount to betraying the sacred connection that she has been able to establish with Parkins and with all that is alive through him. To be kind when ultimate existential issues are at stake amounts to betraying the self and committing harakiri. ". . . I'm not on a stage with actors and dummies any more. Oh, let me pray never to fall back into that bored deadness! After all, I'm like the woman who touched Jesus. You touch the living body, and the flow starts in you, the dead dries up" (p. 85).

There are, however, important differences between the two worlds. Heathcliff adopts a highly solipsistic strategy to preserve the 'carbon' while the Laurentian hero—a Birkin, a Mellors—strives to develop an alternative mode of existence which affirms and enriches rather than denies the affective self. One might even say that the Lawrence hero is an advance upon Heathcliff, i.e., Heathcliff recreated in adult and not-so-solipsistic terms.

Heathcliff lives solely by his passion for Catherine. This is the only way he can relate himself to the world. Towards the end he does seem to betray a little feeling for Hareton, but he promptly kills it to make his defiant exit. Apart from his passion for Catherine, he interacts with the world in two ways. One, he goes about ruthlessly and efficiently demolishing his adversaries—Isabella, Hindley and even his son Linton. This is by no means an autonomous relationship, but only the other side of his passion for Catherine—the negative manifestation of his thwarted eros. Then there is his love of money, his avarice. His avarice, like his revenge, is related to his passion for Catherine and is a sort of pseudo-being. Interestingly, it is Nelly's remark—"It is strange people should be so greedy when they are alone in the world" (p. 75)—that provides the right cue to Heathcliff's lust for money. It is precisely people who are alone need external compensation most—their love of money being a measure of their psychic deprivation. One may recall Karl Marx's observation in *Economic and Philosophic Manuscripts of 1844:* "The less you are, the less you express your own life, the more you have, i.e., the greater is your alienated life, the greater is the state of your estranged being."[13]

While Heathcliff's passion casts a great spell over the reader, and its power is partly because of its solipsism, it must also be admitted that it comes to acquire a negative character towards the end. Heathcliff digging up Catherine's grave and holding her dead body in his arms has an element of necrophilia. Again, Heathcliff tends to become an enemy of the very passion he has lived by when he threatens to turn Hareton out of doors thus linking himself with his oppressor.

For the Laurentian hero too love of the woman is central to his existence, but it does not alienate him from the rest of the world. In fact, it brings him into contact with the world. (In Lawrence's fiction solipsism is a characteristic of the civilized ones like Clifford and Gudrun.) Birkin in *Women in Love* wants to further his relationship with Gerald. Mellors in *Lady Chatterley's Lover*, even finds a job which fulfils rather than denies the affective self and connects him with nature. "I like farming all right. It's not inspiring but then I don't ask to be inspired. I'm used to horses, and cows, though they are very female, have a soothing effect on me. When I sit with my head in her side, milking, I feel very solaced. . . ." (p. 349)

Heathcliff's solipsism is matched by Catherine's emotional regression. A comparison of *Wuthering Heights* with *Lady Chatterley's Lover* would be most instructive. Both Catherine and Connie are caught between men who represent antagonistic ways of living. Also, the polarities represented by these men are nearly the same. Edgar and Clifford represent the claims of culture; Heathcliff and Mellors represent the claims of the passional self. Again, both Catherine and Connie sense the antagonism between the two men and their ways of living, and apprehend it in identical terms. Catherine remarks:

> Whatever our souls are made of his and mine are the same; and Linton's is as different as a moonbeam from lightning, or frost from fire. . . . (*Wuthering Heights*, p. 121).

And about Connie, the author comments:

> She had fugitive dreams of friendship between these two men: one her husband, the other the father of her child. Now she saw the screaming absurdity of her dreams. They mutually exterminated one another. (*Lady Chatterley's Lover*, pp. 223–24)

While both think of bringing the two men together, Connie immediately sees the "absurdity" of it and drops it. Further she comes to realize that she has got to choose between the two as "they mutually exterminated one another". But Catherine cannot resolve the dilemma except in dreams. It is only in her dreams (and reveries) she realizes that she has "no more business to marry Edgar Linton that I have to be in heaven" or she has become "the wife of a stranger". Her waking life, however, is tormented by the division between the conscious and the unconscious and she craves for the integrated life of her childhood. "I wish I were a girl again, half savage and hardy, and free . . ." (p. 163).

In other words Catherine does not have the courage to remould her conscious life in accordance with her dream. Connie responds to the intimations of the life of the body and chooses her destiny accordingly. Lawrence's work thus constitutes an advance on Brontë's. The Brontë dream becomes a reality in his fiction. Or perhaps Brontë is more 'realistic' and knows no way of resolving the eternal strife between the reality principle and the pleasure principle.

* * *

The central affinity between Brontë and Lawrence—their sense of the non-human—manifests itself also in their distinctive use of animal imagery. Hence what follows is a brief analysis of the animal imagery in *Wuthering Heights* and *Women in Love.* Let us look at the following extracts:

> The helpless of an animal was its passport to Charlotte's heart; the fierce, wild intractability of its nature was what often recommended it to Emily?
>
> (Gaskell's *The Life of Charlotte Brontë,* p. 268)

> She (Ursula) loved best of all the animals, that were single and unsociable as she herself was . . . . Each was single and to itself, magical. It was not referred away to some detestable social principle?
>
> (*Women in Love,* p. 275)

If one assumes for a moment that Ursula here represents Lawrence—not an unreasonable assumption I suppose—one would find the similarity between the two novelists striking. Both Brontë and Lawrence love animals and more or less for the same reasons. Brontë for their "fierce intractability", Ursula-Lawrence for their "singleness", i.e., their integrity, their existing in their own right and their refusal to serve extraneous, human ends.

Given their predilections, it is only natural that Brontë and Lawrence should make abundant use of animal imagery. The animal imagery employed by them is not just for heightening an effect, not simply for metaphoric ends; it is centrally related to their world-view, i.e., man must live in close relationship with nature (nature both as an enveloping matrix as well as the passional substratum) and if he sunders himself from it, he will lack authenticity and freedom. The animal imagery becomes a vital means of discovering the other, the dark self that idealistic civilization has fenced out. In the terminology of Lawrence's letter, getting at the "carbon" beneath the diamond surface. For in a world where civilization appropriate human beings for its own ends, animals impervious to human designs become the loci of integrity and freedom.

To be sure, the use of animal imagery is a lot more varied. When a Lawrence protagonist wants to express his/her scorn for somebody he uses the world dog or *canaille* which was incidentally Frieda's favourite expression. One thinks of Gudrun in *Women in Love* when she finds Birkin's bohemian friends reading his letter in the Café Pompadur. " 'I could have killed them!' She cried in passion. 'Dogs!—they are dogs!—' " (p. 435). Also, Birkin expresses his disgust with the cynical Loerke by describing him as "a rat in the river of corruption" (p. 481). Similarly, in *Wuthering Heights,* during the course of a direct confrontation Heathcliff sneers at Edgar and remarks, " 'Cathy—this lamb of yours threatens like a bull' " (p. 153). And when Edgar faints, Catherine goes a step further and contemptuously describes him as a "sucking levert" (p. 154). Such examples can be multiplied, but here I propose to focus on the use of animal imagery as a means of discovering the non-human.

With these two novelists we no longer inhabit an all-too-human world of the traditional English novel where individuals are defined entirely in relation to other human beings. In the fictional world of Brontë and Lawrence the protagonists are delineated to a considerable extent in terms of their response to the non-human world, particularly the animals.

In the very first chapter of *Wuthering Heights* when Heathcliff's dogs attack Lockwood provoked by his "tacit insults", Heathcliff defends them against Lockwood's accusation. Instinctively he—he was not a witness to the scene—knows that the dogs must be in the right. "They won't meddle with persons who touch nothing" (p. 49). One is reminded of Phoenix in "St. Mawr" who refuses to find fault with the horse even though he—Lawrence never uses it for the horse—has overthrown Rico. A little later he suggests that he has more in common with his dogs that with his sophisticated tenant. "Guests are so exceedingly rare in this house that I and my dogs, I am willing to own, hardly know how to receive them" (p. 49).

Animals figure regularly in *Wuthering Heights.* They are a part of the Earnshaw family and when Catherine returns from Thrush cross Grange, "the dogs come bounding up to welcome her" (p. 93). Catherine doesn't want to touch the dogs for she is worried about "her splendid garments?" She is no longer the wild mate of Heathcliff but an elegant lady conscious of her looks and clothes, and this change is communicated in terms of her response to the dogs who come forward to greet her. Also, this pre-figures her alienation, which however is not total, from Heathcliff. Now she finds Heathcliff dirty and "gazes concernedly at the dusky fingers she held in her own own" (p. 95). The scene, apart from reinforcing the link-up between Heathcliff and dogs, effectively establishes that Catherine is now going to be estranged from the passion and spontaneity of her former existence. The equation between dogs and Heathcliff, and then between Heathcliff and Catherine's passional self is established by the apt use of animal imagery.

In Lawrence's "St. Mawr" the leading protagonist in a sense is an animal. St. Mawr the stallion can be said to be the prime mover. Things happen because of him and the leading characters are defined in terms of their response to the horse.

In fact, there is a sharp polarization between those like Rico and the Manbys on the one hand and Lou, Phoenix and Lewis who want to preserve the horse. The former, who may be described as 'humanists', want a safe and sanitized world free from the non-human mystery and danger that St. Mawr represents. Lou, Phoenix and Lewis cannot imagine life without mystery and wonder, and if it also implies danger, so be it; it is a part of the game.

In *Women in Love* animal imagery is employed in a more complex manner. Lawrence, like Brontë, prefigures dominant characteristics of an individual in terms of his or her treatment of the animals. Hermione's bullying nature, against which Birkin revolts, manifests itself in her treatment of the male deer. She talked to the stag "as if he too were a boy she wanted to wheedle and fondle" (p. 97). Similarly in the 'Rabbit' scene is anticipated the see-saw of Gudrun-Gerald affair—its distinctive passion as well as the icy egotistic withdrawal that succeeds it. The 'mad' rabbit becomes a sort of totem of the two protagonists.

Perhaps the most significant scene in the novel from this point of view, i.e., the delineation of characters in terms of their response to the animal, is 'Coal-Dust'. Here Gerald Crich who in a sense is the leading protagonist tries to control the recalcitrant Arab mare—a scene witnessed by the two sisters Ursula and Gudrun.

'Coal-Dust' clearly establishes Gerald's domineering nature by "the mechanical relentlessness" with which he bends her to his will. This domineering nature later manifests itself, in his life as an industrial magnet, in his desire to control the miners. His treatment of the mare is also indicative of his will-ed repression of his own passional self, far Gerald "closed round her and brought her down as if she were part of his own physique" (p. 124). It is Gerald's domineering nature which accounts both far his success as an industrial magnet and failure as a human being, his professional triumph and emotional tragedy.

'Coal-Dust' also delineates Gudrun and Ursula to a great extent. Ursula is revolted by Gerald's attempt "to bully a creature ten times as sensitive as himself". Ursula's naivety, her sensitivity, and the fact that she is a whole-hogger come out clearly in her unequivocal condemnation of Gerald. Gudrun, however, watches him with fascination revealing her sado-masochistic nature. She seems to view the mare as her own surrogate self and derives ecstatic pleasure out of Gerald's attempt to tame the mare. Her dance before the bullocks who serve as Gerald's surrogate self for her, is a kind of sexual challenge flung at Gerald. Together they reveal Gudrun's desire to yield and dominate by turns.

And, finally, a word about the lovers' quarrel in *Wuthering Heights* (Chapter 15) and *Women in Love* ('Excurse'). They are the two most intense love scenes in English fiction. I have already discussed them in some detail earlier in this chapter. All that I wish to emphasize here is that their extraordinary intensity—the Dionysian dimension that they acquire—is owing not a little to the sensitive use of animal imagery. Heathcliff's fierce passion for Catherine and utter indifference to others is communicated by the "mad dog" image. Nelly's alienation (I did not feel as if I were in the company of a creature of my own species . . .) is a measure of the Dionysian nature of the encounter. Similarly, Ursula's eyes "blaze like a tiger". There is something "prophetic" about her wrath. (The tiger image is reminiscent of Blake's poem.) Ursula means to burn the dross of idealistic humbug that Birkin has not been able to free himself from. So similar are these two scenes that it is hard to believe that Lawrence was not influenced by his predecessor.

NOTES AND REFERENCES

1. Quoted from Mark Spilka, *The Love Ethic* of *D. H. Lawrence*, pp. 8–9.
2. Ibid., p. 9.
3. The following observation by Barbara Hardy would seem to vindicate my position, "Emily Brontë anticipates Lawrence's break with the all, stable, moral ego he thought typical of nineteenth century fiction". "Emily and Charlotte Brontë" in *Forms of Feeling in Victorian Fiction* (London: Peter Ownen, 1985), p. 97.
4. *The Letters of D. H. Lawrence,* ed. George J. Zytaruk and James T. Boulton (Cambridge: Cambridge University Press, 1981), II, pp. 182–83.
5. Anthony Burgess' insightful observations on Lawrence's achievement in *Women in Love* can be legitimately applied to *Wuthering Heights* as well:

   "And it is this stripping down which is the essence of the book. The characters are, in their externals, drawn with a delirious sharpness, but they are not human beings as we expect to meet either in real life or in fiction. They are close to animals in the discontinuousness of their emotions, with unpredictable shifts of feeling which are always intense; their unconscious minds are, as in surface mining, a little too close to the light; they are capable of great emotional and even physical violence; they all seem to have a skin missing." *Flame Into Being—The Life and Work of D. H. Lawrence* (London: Heinemann, 1985), p. 89.
6. Another critic who recognizes the kinship between Brontë and Lawrence is Mark Kinkead-Weekes. But he is primarily concerned with the affinities between Catherine and Heathcliff on the one hand and Lawrence protagonists

on the other. "Like all other aspects of their love, it seems to be concerned with a breaking through beyond the self, metaphysical and impersonal as (in Lawrence whom this side of the novel often anticipates)." 'The Place of Love in *Jane Eyre and Wuthering Heights*', The Brontë's: Twentieth Century Views, p. 88.

7. Keith Sagar, *The Art of D. H. Lawrence,* p. 44.
8. 'The Originality of Wuthering Heights', *The Art of Emily Brontë,* ed. Anne Smith (London: The Vision Press, 1976), p. 132.
9. Ibid., p. 150.
10. *The Appropriate Form,* p. 155.
11. Q. D. Leavis seems to take a curious view of the encounter between Catherine and Heathcliff. "Even when Heathcliff is taking farewell of the dying Catherine he upbraids her with her 'infernal selfishness!' " "A Fresh Approach to Wuthering Heights", *Lectures in America,* p. 114.
12. 'Death Is Not Evil, Evil is Mechanical' in *Selected Poems,* Edited with an Introduction by Keith Sagar (Harmondsworth: Penguin, 1972), p. 252.
13. *Collected Works: Karl Marx, F. Engels* (Moscow: Progress Publishers, 1975), p. 309.

Chapter 7

LAWRENCE AND THE COUNTER-CULTURE

LAWRENCE'S VISION OF a non-repressive culture seems vindicated by what has come to be known as counter-culture in the West. That he has been a potent influence on the youth who have tried to break away from "the secular humanist orthodoxy"[1] is generally conceded.[2] I propose to discuss briefly three major 'ideologues' of the counter-culture—Herbert Marcuse, Norman O. Brown and Theodore Roszak to show that their central concerns are basically the same as that of Lawrence, namely, indictment of Western culture for its anthropocentric-rationalistic bias, discovery of the 'wisdom of the body', concern for environment, and even the desire to create a living community as an alternative to the unfeeling Leviathan known as the industrial society. This is not necessarily to suggest that Lawrence influenced them directly, only that he is a kindred spirit—an avant-garde who had the clairvoyance to see that there is a world beyond the *cul de sac* of secular humanism.

It may be recalled that Lawrence indicted Western civilization essentially on two counts: (i) it bullied the passional self, (ii) it alienated man from non-human nature. Marcuse, Brown and Roszak are one with Lawrence in this indictment. Like Lawrence, they too do not view the present crisis in isolation confined to the industrial phase of Western civilization, but as something embedded in the Platonic-Christian legacy. For instance, Marcuse observes in *Eros and Civilization:*

> As the scientific rationality of Western civilization began to bear the full fruit, it became increasingly conscious of its psychical implications. The ego which undertook the rational transformation of the human and natural environment revealed itself as an essentially aggressive, offensive subject, whose thoughts and actions were designed for mastering

> objects. . . . The struggle begins with the perpetual internal conquest of the 'lower' faculties of the individual: his sensuous and appetitive faculties. Their subjugation is, at least since Plato, regarded as a constitutive element of human reason, which is thus in its very function repressive.[3]

Similarly, Norman O. Brown denounces the Platonic ideal as "insane". "For modern secular humanist intellectuals have in the main followed Plato and Descartes over the abyss into the insane delusion that the true essence of man lies in disembodied mental activity."[4]

Thus, for both Marcuse and Brown, as for Lawrence, Plato is the original sinner. Roszak comes to a similar conclusion in *Where the Wasteland Ends.* "Perhaps in all human cultures there has been some tendency to subordinate or bully the body. But I doubt there has been such a hostile breakdown of communication between head and body, such and ingrained, generalised asceticism as ours. . . ."[5]

He reiterates it in an article entitled "In Search of the Miraculous". "It is the uncanny characteristic of western society that so much of our high culture—religion, philosophy, science—has been based on what contemporary therapists would call 'head trips'. . . ."[6]

The counter-culture unequivocally rejects the cardinal principle of Western civilization that man is a soul imprisoned in the body. Norman O. Brown speaks for the entire movement when he identifies the radical element in Freud's thinking:

> Freud is also asserting that in spite of two thousand years of higher education based on the notion that man is essentially a soul for mysterious accidental reasons, imprisoned in a body, man remains incurably obtuse and still secretly thinks of himself as first and foremost a body. Our repressed desires are not just for delight, but specifically for delight in the fulfilment of the life of our bodies.[7]

It is for this reason that both Brown and Marcuse reject monogamous adult sexuality as repressive, and advocate "polymorphous perverse" sexuality. Brown advocates Dionysian consciousness—the consciousness which embraces and affirms the instinctual and thus enables us to live in the present described as "the tense of life". For Brown the affirmation of instinctual reality means not only a complete acceptance of eros but also of death. He comes up with a challenging formulation that the dominion of death in modern man's existence is precisely because he is trying to repress it, and it is this flight from death which results in the denial of life instincts:

> The incapacity to accept death turns the death instinct into its distinctively human and distinctively morbid form. The distraction of human life to the war against death, by the same inevitable irony results in death's dominian over life. The war against death takes the form of a preoccupation with the past and the future, and the present tense, the tense of life, is lost.[8]

It would be interesting to compare Lawrence's position with that of Brown. Lawrence too accepts the necessity of death, even its desirability from a non-human, organic perspective. Death is part of life, and to resist death is to resist life, and to defy the rhythm of nature. It is only people who have "unlived lines in the body", as Rilke would put it, that cling to life even when their time is up. Mrs. Morel in *Sons and Lovers* clings to life and it is seen as something horrible. We may also recall Lawrence's own healthy, even joyous acceptance of death as expressed in his poem 'The Ship of Death':

> Now it is autumn and the falling fruit / and the long journey towards oblivion. / The apples falling like great drops of dew / to bruise themselves an exit from themselves. / And it is time to go, to bid farewell / to one's own self, and find an exit / from the fallen self.[9]

Dorothy Van Ghent is her essay *On Sons and Lovers* lays special emphasis on this aspect of Lawrence's work:

> Perhaps no other modern writer besides Rilke and Mann, has tried so sincerely to bring death into relationship with life, as Lawrence did, and each under the assumption that life, to know itself creatively, must know its relationship with death. . . .[10]

Like Brown, Marcuse also advocates "the resurgence of pregenital polymorphous sexuality", but while for Brown, it is primarily a matter of psychic revolution, the latter sees it from a sociological perspective. Taking his cue from Freud, Marcuse argues that since repression is caused by *ananke,* i.e. scarcity, the attainment of affluence in advanced industrial societies like America would result in a reduction of the working day and an increase of leisure. This is turn would release erotic potentialities. "No longer used as a full-time instrument of labour, the body would be re-sexualized. The regression involved in this spread of the libido would first manifest itself in a reactivation of all erotogenic zones and consequently in a resurgence of pregenital polymorphous sexuality and in a decline of genital supremacy. The body in its entirety would become an object of cathexis, a thing to be enjoyed—an instrument of pleasure."[11] His optimism, however, was considerably eroded when he found that the change in objective conditions did not result in the hoped-for liberation, but on the contrary strengthened the existing structure. "The very forces which rendered society capable of pacifying the struggle for existence served to repress in the individuals the need for such a liberation."[12]

It may not be out of place here to mention Brown's description of D. H. Lawrence as "the paradoxically conservative philosopher of sexuality".[13] Possibly led by Lawrence's reputation as an advocate of phallic consciousness Brown thinks of him as one who idealizes the genital character. This seems a rather superficial view of Lawrence. It is true that Lawrence attaches a lot of significance to orgasm, but it does not imply a devaluation of foreplay, and the gratification derived from the active life of the body. In fact, orgasm in seen as the climax of the gratification derived from an indulgence of the body. Lawrence's emphasis on touch alone establishes the "polymorphous perverse" nature of his sexuality. The relevant discussion in Chapter 5, I hope, established the radical nature of Lawrence's sexuality. Here I would only like to add that Lawrence's approach to aggression is strongly akin to Gestalt therapy:

> An especially significant feature of Gestalt is the dignity it confers on the predatory aspects of human nature. While traditional psychiatry confronts aggressiveness with suspicion or resistance, usually interpreting it as a prime pathological symptom, Gestalt readily embraces it in its natural manifestations and seeks to give it freedom. In Gestalt therapy, the practice is not to talk the patient around and out of the destructive violence he feels within himself, but rather to let him experience it deeply by way of vivid display, so that he might come to accept its necessary presence.[14]

This comes very close to Lawrence's treatment of aggression. I have already talked of the quarrels between Birkin and Ursula in the preceding chapter. (It is useful to remember that the quarrels between Lawrence and Frieda served as the model for this.) Here I shall briefly talk about the therapeutic value that Lawrence attaches to aggression in relationships between men. In *Sons and Lovers,* Lawrence's first important novel, we have the physical fight between Paul Moral and Baxter Dawes which helps them to understand each other better. The wrestling bout between Gerald and Birkin in *Woman in Love* is an even more instructive example. The bout between Birkin and Gerald, helps them release their pent-up frustration and thus recover their sanity. "They stopped, they discussed methods, they practised grips and throws, they became accustomed to each other, to each other's rhythm, they got a kind of mutual physical understanding . . ." (p. 304). Later Birkin remarks that "one ought to wrestle and strive and be physically close. It makes one sane" (p. 307).

Again, Lawrence anticipates to some extent the contemporary concern for environment. Lawrence's last important protagonist Mellors is a gamekeeper who rears pheasants and hates those who shoot them. He shows a living awareness of the non-human world, of horses and cows, and takes to farming. Lawrence himself was opposed to bullying of all sorts, and the ecological crisis of our times can be traced in part at least to the bullying mentality of the West as embodied in the Biblical injunction, "Subdue the earth". As Lymn White points out, "Christianity is the most anthropocentric religion the whole world has ever seen. . . . By destroying pagan animism, Christianity made it possible to exploit nature in a mood of indifference to the feelings of natural objects."[15] The sensitive young men and women in the West seem to be reacting against the ecological bullying which may perhaps explain their interest in oriental religions in general and Zen Buddhism in particular. Roszak's statement in *Where the Wasteland Ends* provides a fair summing up of the contemporary thinking on the issue.

> We forget that nature is quite simply, the universal continuum, ourselves inextricably include; it is that which mothered us into existence, which will out survive us, and from which we have learned (if we still remember the lesson) our destiny. It is the mirror of our identity. Any cultural goods we produce which sunder themselves from this traditional, lively connection with the non-human, any thinking we do which isolates itself from, or pits itself against the natural environment—

> strictly speaking—is a delusion, and a very sick one. Not only because it will lack ecological intelligence, but because it will lack psychological completeness.[16]

Connected with this is the revulsion with the scientific world-view with its reductionist mentality reducing all life to a conjunction of atoms. This must be seen as part of the larger striving to recover the sanctity and wonder of life. Roszak provides a pathological perspective on the reductionist mentality:

> Abraham Maslow has characterised reductionist mentality as a 'cognitive pathology' usually born of fear, rather like a kind of exorcism needed by the chronically distrustful to drive off the menacing spirits. Doubtless in our culture reductionism traces back to the Judeo-Christian mania for desacralizing nature![17]

Lawrence's analysis of the scientific mentality, though similar, is even more devastating. "When the living individual dies, then is the realm of death established. Then you got matter and elements and atoms and forces and sun and moon and earth and stars and so on."[18] Lawrence's entire life and work is a crusade against the "realm of death" and its ambassadors. *Apocalypse* is Lawrence's final affirmation of the magnificent here and now of "life in the flesh" which is also a redpudiation of the "realm of death":

> We ought to dance with rapture that we should be alive and in the flesh, and part of the living, incarnate cosmos. I am part of the sun as my eye is part of me. That I am part of the earth my feet know perfectly, and my blood is part of the sea.[19]

Finally, the young all over Western Europe and America are engaged in a search for an authentic community that would replace the impersonal, dehumanizing leviathan called industrial society, a community which would take the individual into account. "In a world which more and more thinks of society as the subordinate adjunct of a gigantic technological mechanism the young begin to speak of such impracticalities as 'community' and 'participative democracy'. Thus they revert to a style of human relations that characterize village and tribe, insisting that real politics can take place in the deeply personal confrontations these now obsolete social forms allow. . . . The lively consciousness of men and women as they are in their vital daily reality is missing from our culture, having been displaced by these grandiose figments. . . .'[20]

"The lively consciousness of men and women as they are." Would not that be an apt description of the ideal community that Lawrence wanted to build? Even his misanthropy is a measure of his revulsion with men who reduced themselves to functions in an industrial machine robbing themselves of joy and wonder without which there can be no living community. Lawrence discovered that the primitive cultures—the Mexicans and the Etruscans—knew the art of living better than the industrial West which equated living with getting and spending. As opposed to the cerebral-mechanical relationships of the industrial West, Lawrence envisages vital organic relationships as the warp and woof of the living community. In a letter to Rolf Gardner, Lawrence wrote:

> I think, one day, I shall take a place in the country, somewhere where perhaps one or two other men might like to settle in the neighbourhood, and we might possibly slowly evolve a new rhythm of life: learn to make the creative pauses, and learn to dance and to sing together, without stunting, and perhaps also publish some little fighting periodical, keeping fully aware alert and alive to the world, living a different life in the midst of it, not merely apart. . . . One needs to establish a fuller relationship between oneself and the universe, and between oneself and one's fellow men and women. It does not mean cutting out the brothers-in-Christ business simply; it means expanding it into a full relationship, where there can be also physical and passional meeting, as there used to be in the old dances and rituals. We have to know how to go out and meet one another, upon the third ground, the holy ground.[21]

Here we have the salient features of Lawrence's living community—his Rananim (i) his utopia is not an escapist retreat, for it means "living a different life in the midst of it, not merely apart"; (ii) the emphasis on physical and passional meeting which the ideal West distrusts, and the related emphasis on group dances which make such contact possible; (iii) the fuller relationship with oneself and one's fellowmen implies an awareness of the non-human.

In *Lady Chatterley's Lover,* Lawrence's protagonist Mellors makes the same point in his naive way:

> They ought to learn to be naked and handsome, and to sing in a mass and dance the old group dances, and carve the stools they sit on, and embroider their own emblems. Then they wouldn't need money. And that is the only way to solve the industrial problem; train the people to be able to live and live in handsomeness, without needing to spend. . . . They should be alive and frisky and acknowledge the great God Pan. (p. 351)

Apart from the usual Laurentian emphasis on "the old group dances" and singing together, we have here the plea for interacting with the environment through organic, personal work "carve the stools they sit on, and embroider their own emblems" as against alienated, industrial work which makes the industrial men so pathetically dependent on money. Lawrence sees money as the industrial disease or the symptom of a disease. The industrial man's obsession with spending money results from his lack of fulfulment in his work and relationship. The more alienated one is the more is the compulsion to spend. Mammon is the god of the damned—of those who have lost their bodies. Against Mammon, Lawrence advances the claims of Pan. It would appear that taking the cue from Lawrence young men and women, in Europe and America are striving to build a world where Pan would replace Mammon. Obviously, the success of such striving in a Mammon-dominated world can at best be partial.

NOTES AND REFERENCES

1. Theodore Roszak, "In Search of the Miraculous" *Span* (December, 1981), p. 12.
2. "Lawrence has been a major influence on the social attitude which has grown up in the United States since the Second World War and which may be described as a development of Freudianism. Freud himself had little hope that society would ever cease to be a repressive anxiety-structure, but some of the most uninhibited utopian thinking today comes from such Freudians as Norman O. Brown (*Life Against Death*) and Herbert Marcuse (*Eros and Civilisation*), who urge us at least to consider the possibility of a non-repressive society!" Northrop Frye, *Daedalus*, 94 (1965), p. 346.
3. *Eros and Civilization* (1969; rpt London: Sphere Books, 1970), p. 96.
4. *Life Against Death*, p. 34.
5. *Where the Wasteland Ends* (New York: Doubleday and Company, 1972), p. 97.

6. *Span*, p. 13.

Earlier, writing in a similar vein, Lawrence had denounced 'Know They Self' as a 'risky motto':

> We want *effectual* human beings, not conscious ones. The final aim is not to *know*, but to *be*. There never was a more risky motto than that: Know thyself. . . . 'Be Yourself' is the last motto.

Fantasia of the Unconscious in *Fantasia of the Unconscious* and *Psychoanalysis of The Unconscious* (Harmondsworth: Penguin, 1971), p. 68.

7. *Life Against Death*, p. 31.
8. Ibid., p. 284.
9. *Selected Poems*, ed. Keith Sagar (1972; rpt Harmondsworth: Penguin, 1975), p. 253.
10 *D. H. Lawrence: Twentieth Century Views*, ed. Mark Spilka, p. 28.
11. *Eros and Civilization*, pp. 163–64.
12. 'Political Preface 1966', *Eros and Civilization*, p. 11.
13. *Life Against Death*, p. 181.
14. Theodore Roszak, *The Making of a Counter-Culture* (1971: rpt London: Faber & Faber, 1973), p. 193.
15. Quoted from *Where The Wasteland Ends*, p. 126.
16. Ibid., p. 7.
17. Ibid., p. 264.
18. *Fantasia of the Unconscious* in *Fantasia of the Unconscious* and *Psychoanalysis and The Unconscious* (1971; rpt Harmondsworth: Penguin, 1973), p. 151.
19. *Apocalypse*, p. 126.
20. *The Making of a Counter-Culture*, p. 54.
21. *The Collected Letters of D. H. Lawrence*, II, pp. 940–41.

CODA

AS WE HAVE seen, Rousseau, Nietzsche, Freud, Brontë, Lawrence (and later Brown and Roszak) find Western civilization repressive as it sacrifices the body to the mind, the present to the future, spontaneity to foresight, and happiness to progress. Lawrence said science, Socrates and Christ—all murder the flesh. To this one may also add Marxism—the last deity to arrive on the Western scene. For the Marxist millennium is only the secular analogue of the Christian kingdom of heaven. This earthly paradise too is not here in the present, in the palm of one's hand, but somewhere in the future. No wonder, youth in France and elsewhere have dismissed orthodox Marxism as "une revolution à la papa".[1] Keynes once described capitalism as a case of "jam tomorrow".[2] This could in fact be said of Western civilization as a whole: its jam-tomorrowism manifests itself in Christian heaven and Marxist utopia alike.

This however constitutes a denial of life in the present which, as Norman O. Brown observed, is 'the tense of life',[3] and to live is to live, first and foremost, in the body. The body bullied and denied takes its revenge like the stallion in Lawrence's novella "St. Mawr" and the bloody history of the West bears dramatic testimony to the consequences that follow from repression of the animal. Nietzsche, Freud, Lawrence and Brontë—notwithstanding important differences between them—show an acute awareness of the 'impossibility' of Western, Christian ethic, its utter estrangement from the affective self.

Hence, both Brontë and Lawrence make a plea for a different treatment of the dark self—Plato's black horse—for an unself conscious acceptance of the erotic and the aggressive. To come to terms with the animal makes for wholeness of being and happiness, while to bully it and fence it out makes for disaster. In this sense the 'primitives' like Heathcliff and Mellors are superior to Cliffords and

Lockwoods. Significantly, cruelty of the 'civilized' figures rather prominently in both Brontë and Lawrence. It is a measure of the inadequacy of idealistic civilization and also its indictment.

There is, however, an important difference between Brontë and Lawrence. While the Brontë protagonists preserve the passional self through solipsistic or regressive defences, Lawrence envisages a societal form which would fulfil rather than deny it. Hence Lawrence's emphasis on group-dances and handicraft and farming. While group-dances are meant to connect men with their fellow beings, handicrafts and farming bring them into a living relationship with the environment.

In Brown, Roszak and Marcuse we find the quest for a non-repressive civilization—a civilization which would neither main the self nor alienate man from nature, a civilization grounded in the wisdom of the body, and a reverence for non-human environment. That is why young men and women in Western Europe and America, looking for a living alternative to the unfeeling industrial machine, turned to them.

Finally, even though Christian motto "man is the lord of creation" has got somewhat discredited in the west, it continues to inspire the ruling elites of the 'third world' resulting in merciless plunder of nature. The 'protestant' vision of Brontë and Lawrence is, therefore, of even greater relevance to them.

NOTES AND REFERENCES

1. One of the May 1968 slogans reads as follows: "Une revolution qui demande que l'on se sacrifice pour ille est une revolution à la papa." (A revolution that expects you to sacrifice yourself for it is one of daddy's revolutions.)

   Cited in Roszak's *The Making of a Counter-Culture* (London: Faber & Faber, 1970), p. 58.
2. The repressiveness implicit in "jam tomorrow" is adequately spelt out in the following observation, "The purposive man is always trying to secure a spurious and delusive immortality for his acts by pushing his interest in the them forward into time. . . . For him jam is not jam unless it is a case of jam tomorrow and never jam today". "Economic Possibilities For Our Grandchildren" in *Essays in Persuasion: The Collected Writings of John Maynard Keynes*, p. 330.
3. *Life Against Death*, p. 284.

BIBLIOGRAPHY

Allott, Miriam. "The Rejection of Heathcliff?" *Emily Brontë: Wuthering Heights—A Case-book*, ed. Miriam Allott. London & Basingstoke: MacMillan 1970, pp. 183–206.

Babbitt, Irving. *Rousseau and Romanticism.* Boston & New York: Houghton Miffin Comp., 1968.

Blondel, Jacques. "The Role of Nature in Emily Brontë's Poetry." *Emily Brontë: Penguin Critical Anthologies*, ed. Jean-Pierre Petit. Harmondsworth: Penguin, 1973, pp. 135–50.

Brontë, Emily. *Five Essays Written in French by Emily Jane Brontë*, trans. Lorine White Nagel, with an Introduction & Notes by Fannie F. Ratchford. University of Texas Press, 1948.

———, *Gondal's Queen.* Arranged by Fannie E. E. Ratchford. University of Texas Press, 1955.

———, *Gondal Poems,* ed. Helen Brown & Joan Mott. Oxford: Basil Blackwell, 1973.

———, *Wuthering Heights.* Harmondsworth: Penguin, 1965.

Brown, Norman O. *Life Against Death.* New York: Random House, 1959.

Buchen, Irving H. "Emily Brontë and the Metaphysics of Childhood and Love." *Emily Brontë: Penguin Critical Authology*, ed. Jean-Pierre Petit. Harmondsworth: Penguin, 1973, pp. 248–55.

Burgess, Anthony. *Flame Into Being—The Life and Work of D.H. Lawrence.* London: Heinemann, 1985.

Burns, Aidan. *Nature and Culture in D.H. Lawrence.* London & Basing Stoke: MacMillan, 1980.

Cassirer, Ernst. *An Essay on Man.* New Haven: Yale University Press, 1945.

———, *The Philosophy of Symbolic Forms,* trans. Ralph Manheim. 3 Vols. New Haven: Yale University Press, 1955.

Cecil, David. "Emily Brontë and Wuthering Heights." *Emily Brontë: Penguin Critical Anthology*. Harmondsworth: Penguin, 1973, pp. 92–98.

Copleston, F. *Friedrich Nietzsche Philosopher of Culture.* 1942; rpt. London: Search Press & New York: Barnes & Noble Books, 1975.

Daleski, H. M. *The Forked Flame—A Study of D. H. Lawrence.* London: Faber & Faber, 1965.

Dix, Carol. *D. L. Lawrence and Women.* London: MacMillan, 1980.

Donoghue, Denis. "Emily Brontë: On the Latitude of Interpretation." *Emily Brontë: Penguin Critical Anthology.* Harmondsworth: Penguin, 1973, pp. 296–325.

Drabble, Margaret. *A Writer's Britain: Landscape in Literature.* London: Thames & Hudson, 1979.

Drain, Richard. "Women in Love." *D. H. Lawrence,* ed. A. H. Gomme. Sussex: Harvester Press, 1979, pp. 70–93.

Eliot, T. S. *Notes Towards the Definition of Culture.* London: Faber & Faber, 1962.

Frank, Katherine. *Emily Brontë: A Chainless Soul.* London: Hamish Hamilton, 1990.

Freud, Sigmund. *Collected Papers,* trans. Joan Riviere, 1925; rpt. London: Hogarth Press, IV, 1953.

——, *The Major Works of S. Freud,* trans. Joan Riviere. *Great Books of The Western World,* ed. R.M. Hutchins Chicago: Encyclopedia Britannica.

——, *The Future of an Illusion,* trans. W.D. Robson-Scott. London: Hogarth Press, 1934.

Gaskall, Elizabeth. *The Life of Charlotte Brontë,* ed. Alan Shelston. Harmondsworth: Penguin, 1975.

Gerin, Winifred. *Emily Brontë: A Biography.* Oxford, New York, Melbourne: Oxford University Press, 1978.

Ghent, Dorothy Van. "Wuthering Heights." *Emily Brontë:* Penguin Critical Anthologies, ed. Jean-Pierre Petit. Harmondsworth: Penguin, 1973, pp. 116–23.

——, "On Sons & Lovers." *D.H. Lawrence: Twentieth Century Views,* ed. Mark Spilka. New Jersey: Prentice Hall, 1963, pp. 15–28.

Goodheart, Eugene. *The Utopian Vision of D.H. Lawrence.* Chicago: University of Chicago Press, 1963.

——, *The Cult of the Ego.* Chicago & London: University of Chicago Press, 1968.

Hardy, Barbara. *The Appropriate Form.* 1964; rpt. London: Athlone Press, 1971, pp. 132–73.

——, *Wuthering Heights.* Blackwell, 1963.

Hardy, Barbara. "Emily and Charlotte Brontë." *Forms of Feeling in Victorican Fiction.* London: Peter Owen, 1985, pp. 97–104.

Hough, Graham. *The Dark Sun.* London: Gerald Duckworth, 1956.

Johnson, Lesley. *The Cultural Critics From Mathew Arnold to Raymond Williams.* London: Routledge & Kegan Paul, 1979.

Jung, Carl. "Role of the Unconscious." *Civilisation in Transition*, trans. R.F.C. Hull 1964; rpt. London: Routledge & Kegan Paul, 1974, pp. 3–28.

Jung, Carl. "Apollonian and Dionysian." *Phsysiological Types*, trans. R.F.C. Hull, 1964; rpt. London: Routledge & Kegan Paul, 1974, pp. 170–83.

Kaufmann, Walter. "Nietzsche." *Encyclopedia of Philosophy*. Vol V, ed-in-chief Paul Edwards, New York: MacMillan, 1967.

———, *Nietzsche Philosopher, Psychologist, Antichrist*. Princeton; New Jersey, 1974.

Kazin, Alfred. "The Freudian Revolution Analysed." *Freud and the 20th Century*, ed. & Sel. Benjamin Nelson, New York: Meridian, pp. 13–21.

Kermode, Frank. *Lawrence*. Collins: Fontana, 1973.

Kettle, Arnold. "Wuthering Heights." *An Introduction to the English Novel*. 1953, rpt. London: Hutchinson University, Library, 1965, I, pp. 139–55.

Keynes, J. M. "Economic Possibilities for Our Grand Children." *Essays in Persuasion: The Collected Writings of John Maynard Keynes*. 1931; rpt. London & Basingstokes MacMillan, 1972, pp. 321–32.

Kinkead-Weekes, M. "The Place of Love in Jane Eyre & Wuthering Heights." *The Brontës: Twentieth Century Views*, ed. Ian Gregor. New Jersey: Prentice Hall, 1970, pp. 76–95.

Lawrence, D. H. *Apocalypse*. Harmondsworth: Penguin, 1971.

———, "A'Propos of Lady Chatterley's Lover." *A Selection from Phoenix*, ed. A.A.H. Inglis. Harmondsworth: Penguin, 1979, pp. 327–61.

———, *The Letters of D. H. Lawrence*, ed. George J. Zytaruk and James T. Boulton. Cambridge: Cambridge University Press, 1981, Vol II.

———, *The Letters of D. H. Lawrence*, ed. James T. Boulton and Lindeth Vasey. Cambridge: Cambridge University Press, 1989, Vol.V.

———, *Fantasia of the Unconscious* and *Psychoanalysis and The Unconscious*. Harmondsworth: Penguin, 1971.

———, *The First Lady Chatterley*. Harmondsworth: Penguin, 1973.

———, *John Thomas & Lady Jane*. Harmondsworth: Penguin, 1977.

———, *Kangaroo*. Harmondsworth: Penguin, 1950.

———, *Lady Chatterley's Lover*. New York: Cardinal, 1959.

———, *The Lost Girl*. Harmondsworth: Penguin, 1950.

———, *Mornings in Mexico* and *Etruscan Places*. Harmondsworth: Penguin, 1960.

———, *The Plumed Serpent*. Harmondsworth: Penguin, 1950.

———, *The Rainbow*. Harmondsworth: Penguin, 1949.

——, *Selected Poems,* ed. Keith Sagar. Harmondsworth: Penguin, 1972.

——, *St. Mawr and The Virgin and the Gypsy.* Harmondsworth: Penguin, 1950.

——, *Studies in Classic American Literature.* Harmondsworth: Penguin, 1971.

——, *Sun* in *The Women Who Rode Away* and *Other Stories.* Harmondsworth: Penguin, 1950.

——, *The White Peacock.* Harmondsworth: Penguin, 1950.

——, *Women in Love,* Harmondsworth: Penguin, 1960.

Leavis, F. R. *D. H. Lawrence—Novelist.* Harmondsworth: Penguin, 1964.

——, "The Orthodoxy of Enlightenment." *Anna Karenia & Other Essays.* London: Chatto & Windus, 1967, pp. 235–41.

Leavis, Q. D. "A Fresh Approach to Wuthering Heights." *Lectures in America* (F. R. & Q. D. Leavis). London: Chatto & Windus, 1969, pp. 83–152.

Lovejoy, Arthur. "The Supposed Primitivism of Rousseau's *Discourse on Inequality.*" *Modern Philology,* 21 (1923-24), pp. 165–86.

Lovejoy, Arthur & Boas, George. *A Documentary History of Primitivism & Relates Ideas.* Baltimore: John Hopkins Press, 1935.

Maddox, Brenda. *The Married Man—A Life of D. H. Lawrence.* London: Sinclair-Stevenson, 1914.

Marcuse, Herbert. *Eros and Civilization.* London: Sphere Books, 1969.

Marx, Karl. "Economic & Philosophic Manuscripts." *Collected Works: Karl Marx, F. Engels.* Moscow: Progress Publishers, 1975, III, pp. 231–346.

Meyers, Jeffrey. *D. H. Lawrence and the Experience of Italy.* Philadelphia: University of Pennsylvania, 1982.

Meyers, Jeffrey. *D. H. Lawrence and Tradition.* London: Athlone Press, 1985.

Miller, Henry. *The World of Lawrence,* ed. Evelyn J. Hinz & John J. Jeunissen. London: John Calder, 1985.

Miller, J. Hillis. *The Disappearance of God.* Cambridge: Harvard University Press, 1963.

Moser, Thomas. "What is the Matter with Emily Jane? Conflicting Impulse in *Wuthering Heights.*" Nineteenth Century Fiction, 17 (1962), pp. 1–19.

Moynahan, Julian. *The Deed of Life.* New Jersey: Princeton University Press, 1963.

——, "Pastoralism as Culture & Counter-Culture in English Fiction 1800-1928." *Towards A Poetics of Fiction—Essays from Novel: A*

Forum on Fiction, 1967-76, ed. Mark Spilka. Bloomington & London: Indiana University Press, 1977, pp. 239–54.

Muggeridge, Malcolm. *Jesus The Man Who Lives.* London: Collins, St. James Place, 1975.

Mumford, Lewis. *Technics & Civilization.* London: Routledge & Kegan Paul, 1967.

Nahal, Chaman. *D. H. Lawrence: An Eastern View.* Delhi: Atma Ram & Sons, 1971.

Niebuhr, H. Richard. *Christ & Culture.* London: Faber and Faber, 1952.

Nietzsche, F. *Twilight of the Idols & The Anti Christ,* trans. R. J. Hollingdale. Harmondsworth: Penguin, 1968.

———, *Genealogy of Morals* in *The Philosophy of Nietzsche,* trans. Horance B. Samuel. 1927; rpt New York: Random House, 1959.

O'Brien, Kate. "Diaries & Journals." *The Heritage of British Literature.* E. Bowen, D. Cecil, G. Green, Kate O'Brien. London: Thames & Hudson, 1983, pp.161-217.

Paglia, Camille. *Sex and Violence, or Nature And Art.* London: Penguin 60s, 1995.

Paz, Octavio. "The Revolt of the Body." *Hudson Review,* 23 (1970–71), pp. 648–65.

Plato, *Dialogues of Plato,* trans. Benjamin Jowett. *Great Books of the Western World,* ed. Robert M. Hutchins. Chicago: Encyclopedia Britannica, 1952.

Pykett, Lyn. *Emily Brontë.* London: MacMillan, 1989.

Rahv, Philip. "On F.R. Leavis and D.H. Lawrence." *Literature and the Sixth Sense.* London: Faber & Faber, 1970, pp. 287–306.

Rieff, Philip. *Freud: The Mind of the Moralist.* New York: Viking Press, 1959.

Roszak, Theodore. *Where the Wasteland Ends.* New York: Doubleday & Company, 1972.

———, *The Making of a Counter-Culture.* 1971; rpt. London: Faber & Faber, 1973.

———, "In Search of the Miraculous". *Span,* Dec. 1981, pp. 10-15.

Rougemont, Denis De. *Passion and Society,* trans. Montgomery Betejian. London: Faber & Faber, 1956.

Rousseau, J.J. *Social Contract and Discourses,* trans. G.D.H. Cole. New York: E. P. Dulton & Co., 1950.

———, *French and English Philosophers,* ed. Charles. W. Eliot. Collier: Harvard Classics, 1938.

———, *The Indispensable Rousseau,* comp. John Hope Mason. London: Quarter Books, 1979.

Sagar, Keith. *The Life of D. H. Lawrence—An Illustrated Biography.* London: Eyre Methuen, 1980.

——, *Art of D. H. Lawrence.* Cambridge: Cambridge University Press, 1966.

——, "The Originality of Wuthering Heights." *The Art of Emily Brontë*, ed. Anne Smith. London: Vision Press, 1976, pp. 121–59.

Sibley, Mulford. *Nature and Civilization: Some Implications for Politics.* Illinois: F.E. Peacock Publishers, Itasca, 1977.

Spilka, Mark. *The Love Ethic of D. H. Lawrence.* London: Dennis Dobson, 1958.

——, *D. H. Lawrence: Twentieth Century Views*, ed. & intro. Mark Spilka. New Jersey: Prentice Hall, 1963.

Steiner, George. *In Bluebeard's Castle: Some Notes Towards the Redefinition of Culture.* London: Faber and Faber, 1974.

Stern, J.P. *A Study of Nietzsche.* Cambridge, London, New York, Melbourne: Cambridge University Press, 1979.

Thompson, Wade. "Infanticide & Sadism in Wuthering Heights." *Emily Brontë: Penguin Critical Anthology*, ed. Jean Pierre Petit. Harmondsworth: Penguin, 1973, pp. 193–204.

Visick Mary. "From The Genesis of Wuthering Heights." *Emily Brontë: Penguin Critical Anthology*, ed. Jean-Pierre Petit. Harmondsworth: Penguin, 1973, pp. 163–79.

Vivas, Eliseo. *D. H. Lawrence: The Failure and the Triumph of Art.* London: George Allen & Unwin, 1961.

Wallace, Robert. *Emily Brontë and Beethoven.* Georgia: University of Georgia Press, 1986.

Watson, Melvin "Wuthering Heights and the Critics." *Nineteenth Century Fiction*, 3(1949), pp. 243–63.

Williams, Linda. *Victorian Literature from 1830 to 1900*, ed. Jane Thomas. London: Bloomsbury, 1994.

Williams, Raymond. *Culture and Society 1780-1950.* London: Chatto & Windus, 1958.

INDEX

Babbitt, Irving 25n
Barbellion, Wilhelm Nero Pilate 26n
Bataille, Georges 41n
Blondel, Jacques 41n
Brontë, Charlotte 10, 19, 33, 41n
Brontë, Emily 13, 19–21; *Wuthering Heights* 2-4, 6, 9-10, 28-40, 41n–42n, 80–82; Gondal Romance 41n; "No Coward Soul Is Mine" 42n; *Five Essays Written in French* 43n; Brontë compared to Lawrence 42n, 44, 78-80, 95n, 105-6; *Wuthering Heights* compared to *Women in Love* 84–6, 90–4; *Wuthering Heights* compared to *Lady Chatterley's Lover* 87–90; *Wuthering Heights* compared to "St. Mawr" 34, 47, 92.
Brown, Norman O. 8, 11, 25n, 96–9, 105.
Burgess, Anthony 94,
Burns, A. 8
Bullock, F. A. 5

Cassirer, Ernst 23–4
Cecil, David 1–2
Chase, Richard 1–3, 40
Copleston, F. 26n

Daleski, H. M. 58
De Nitto, Dennis 8
Dobell, Sidney 4–5
Drain, Richard 57

Frank, Katherine 41n
Freud, Sigmund 17–9, 27n, 43n, 97

Gaskell, Elizabeth 26n, 42n, 90
Ghent, Dorothy Van 5, 98
Goodheart, Eugene 7–8

Harding, D. W. 48
Hardy, Barbara 66, 71, 84–5, 94n
Hough, Graham 50–2, 61

Jones, Ernest 25n
Jung, Carl 23, 29, 41n

Kettle, Arnold 1, 3, 32
Keynes, J. M. 49, 105, 106n
Kinkead-Weekes, Mark 1, 9–10, 94n

Lawrence, D. H. 6–8, 13, 22–5, 64, 82–3, 96, 98–103, 105–6; *Women in Love* 50–62, 68–70, 83–4; *Lady Chatterley's Lover* 47–9, 66–7; *The First Lady Chatterley* 65–6, 71–2; "St Mawr" 46–7, 74–6; *The Rainbow* 44–6; "Sun" 73–4; *Sons and Lovers* 66, 73, 100; *The Letters of D. H. Lawrence* 22, 64, 102; *Apocalypse* 21–3, 72, 101; *Phoenix—The Posthumous Papers of D. H. Lawrence* 59, 70; *Fantasia of the Unconscious* in *Fantasia of the Unconscious* and *Psychoanalysis and the Unconscious* 101, 104n

Leavis, F. R. 6, 48, 58, 62, 74, 80
Leavis, Q. D. 1, 3–4, 42n, 95n
Lovejoy, Arthur 25n

Maddox, Brenda 12n, 76n
Marcuse, Herbert 96–9
Marx, Karl 49, 88–9
Melville, Herman 37, 81
Meyers Jeffrey 11n
Miller, J. Hillis 1–2, 28–9, 32–3
Moynahan, Julian 5–6, 50

Niebuhr, H. Richard 23
Nietzsche 15–7, 20, 27n, 36

Paglia, Camille 27n
Paz, Octavio 51
Plato 15–6, 46, 49, 65, 97
Pykett, Lyn 12n, 41n

Roszak, Theodore 8, 11, 96, 97, 100–1, 106n

Rousseau 13–5, 25n
Russell, Bertrand 22

Sagar, Keith 1, 7, 9, 80
Spilka, Mark 68, 73, 78
Steiner, George 27n

Taine, Hippolyte 78

Vivas, Eliseo 48, 64

Wallace, Robert 43n
Williams, Linda 42n
Williams, Raymond 50
White, Lymn 27n, 100